KARIN MIZGALA
SHEILA WALKINGTON

YOUR MONEY MAP

How to plan and organize your

money to create your ideal life.

MONEY
COACHES
CANADA

Taking the worry out of money
www.moneycoachescanada.ca

Table of Contents

Your Money Map Program

What's Your Starting Point? 2
Taking the Worry Out of Money 4
Money Coaches Canada 4
Your Money Map. 6
Our goals for this program are to: 6
Your role: 6
What are your goals for the program? 7

Dream

What You Really Really Want 11

It's Your Life. 13
The Power Behind The Plan. 13
A Plan Begins With A Dream 14
YOUR DREAMS. 15
Goals Are The Photo Ops Of Your Future 16
Measurable, Achievable & True 17
Time and Money 17
Goal Setting Hints 18
YOUR LIFE AND FINANCIAL GOALS 19
Commitment 20
Creative Ways to Think About Balancing Conflicting Goals 20
Review and Revise 23

You and Your Money. 24
Uncovering the Unconscious: Unmixing the Mixed Messages 26
WHAT DID YOUR PARENTS TEACH YOU ABOUT MONEY? 27
WHAT DOES MONEY MEAN FOR YOU? 30

Blocks to Financial Success 31
Obstacles You Can Overcome 32
Claiming Your Financial Power 34
Just Do Your Best 34
YOUR TOP 3 GOALS! 35

Plan

Your Financial Starting Point. 39
Give Yourself The Freedom to Choose. 39
Net Worth 40
THE DETAILS FOR YOUR NET WORTH STATEMENT 41
YOUR NET WORTH STATEMENT. 42
Cash Flow 43
Instructions for Completing the Cash Flow Worksheet. 44
YOUR CASH FLOW. 45
Interpreting the Numbers 46
Turning The Numbers Into Conscious Choices 47
Consciously Create a Spending and Savings Plan 48
Instructions for Completing the Spending and Savings Plan 48

Hints on Setting Reasonable Targets 48
YOUR SPENDING AND SAVING PLAN. 50
Even Changes Can Change 51

On Track Money Management System. 52
Budget Blues 52
On Track Money Management System 53
Implementing the On Track Money Management System 55
ANNUAL OR LUMP SUM EXPENSES WORKSHEET. 60

Make Savings A Habit. 62
You Just Have to Save 62
Hints On Setting Reasonable Savings Goals 63
Creative Ways To Save. 63
Put Your Savings Goals In Your Spending and Savings Plan. 64

You and Your Credit 65
A Good Credit History is Important 65
Responsible Debt Management 66
Good Debt vs. Bad Debt. 67
Trust Your Plan 68
Get Out of Debt. 68
Creative Ways to Get Out and Stay Out of Debt 69
Instructions for Setting a Debt-Free Date 70
Put Your Debt Repayment Goals In Your Spending and Savings Plan 71

Invest in Yourself. 72
A Quick Word About Risk 73
What Your Money Can Do For You. 74
Investing with Class 74
The Risk-Return Trade-Off 76
An Easy Way In 76
A Note On Real Estate 78
What is Your Money Doing For You? 79
Instructions to Complete the Current Investment Worksheets 79
Hints for Completing the Current Investment Worksheets 79
YOUR CURRENT REGISTERED INVESTMENTS 80
YOUR CURRENT NON-REGISTERED INVESTMENTS. 81
Dividing Up Your Investment Dollars 82
Again, It Goes Back To Your Goals. 83
Instructions For Creating Goal-Centred Investment Plans 85
Asset Class and Asset Allocation Summary 85
WHICH INVESTMENTS ARE RIGHT FOR ME? 86
A Few Thoughts On Strategy 89
Investment Tools You Can Use. 90
Who To Trust With Your Investment Dollars 91
The Do-It-Yourself Approach. 91
Who Can Help You? How Can They Help? And How Do They Get Paid? 91
Fees to ask about. 93
How to Interview a Potential Advisor 94
Review and Rebalance. 95
INVESTING NEXT STEPS? 96

It's Tax Time 97
Canadians are Progressive 97
Tax Talk. 99

Tax Planning 99
Not All Income is Taxed Equally 100
How to Minimize Your Tax Bill 103
Common Questions 103
TAX PLANNING NEXT STEPS 106

A Retirement Planning Primer 107
The 3 Biggest Retirement Mistakes You Don't Want to Make 108
A Framework for the Plan 108
What Does Retirement Mean to You? 108
YOUR RETIREMENT VISION 109
YOUR RETIREMENT GOALS 110
How much money will you need to live? 110
YOUR RETIREMENT LIFESTYLE EXPENSES 111
Where Will My Income Come From? 112
ESTIMATING YOUR INCOME 114
How Much More Do I Have To Save? (Otherwise known as Gap Management.) 115
Review, Revise and Take Action 116
RETIREMENT PLANNING NEXT STEPS? 117

Insurance Basics 118
You Can Be Self-Insured 119
Get Your Money's Worth 119
Typical Times To Review Your Insurance Needs 120
Life Insurance 121
Disability Insurance 123
Critical Illness Insurance 124
Long Term Care Insurance 125
WHAT ARE YOUR BASIC INSURANCE NEEDS? 126
YOUR INSURANCE INVENTORY 127
Review, Revise and Take Action 128

Put Your Estate In Order 129
What is Estate Planning? 130
HOW DO YOU WANT TO BE REMEMBERED? 131
Make Your Wishes Clear 132
Probate 133
Who Will Speak For You When You Can No Longer Speak For Yourself? 134
Talk While You Still Can 136
Further Research 136
CLARIFY AND COMMUNICATE YOUR WISHES 137
Your Estate Planning Action Plan 138

Live It!

Take Action 140
Stand Firmly On Your Accomplishments To Reach Your Goals 141
Take Conscious Action Now 142
YOUR MONEY MAP CHECKLIST 143
ACTION PLAN 144
Review and Revise 145
Keep Up the Good Work 145
Remember the Secret 147
MY ANNUAL REVIEW CHECKLIST 148

Your Money Map

What's Your Starting Point?

	Yes	No	Don't Know
Have you written down your Life and Financial Goals?	☐	☐	☐
Do you know what your Net Worth is?	☐	☐	☐
Do you feel in control of your spending?	☐	☐	☐
Are you satisfied with your savings habits?	☐	☐	☐
Do you ever worry about being financially dependent on others?	☐	☐	☐
Do you pay your credit cards in full every month?	☐	☐	☐
Do you have investments?	☐	☐	☐
Do you feel confident about how your money is invested?	☐	☐	☐
Do you have a good understanding of your pension and insurance programs at work?	☐	☐	☐
Are you saving for your retirement every year?	☐	☐	☐
Do you know how much money you will need for retirement?	☐	☐	☐
Do you worry about not having enough?	☐	☐	☐
Do you have RSPs?	☐	☐	☐
Do you know what pension and government benefits you will receive?	☐	☐	☐
Are you confident that you have appropriate insurance coverage?	☐	☐	☐
Do you have a will or have you written any instructions for your estate?	☐	☐	☐
Do you know what you need to do financially to live your ideal life?	☐	☐	☐

Take a Deep Breath,
Release the Worry,
You'll Have a Plan.

Your Money Map will prepare you to live *well* with your money (both the money you have now and the money you will have in the future).

You are about to build your financial know-how. You will take time to appreciate and admire the life you want. You are going to let go of the blockages that hold you back financially. And in the process, you will create a plan to live a fabulous life - your life!

Just so you're not waiting for it, we've put the secret to your financial success right up front. This is it:

The real key to financial satisfaction is aligning the money you have (and will have) with your values, aspirations and goals.

Starting now you are going to:

>   use your goals to motivate you to take control of your money.

As soon as you start working your plan you are going to:

>   use your money to achieve your goals and

>   use your goals to motivate you to keep control of your money.

Here's another secret. Once a basic level of financial stability is established, there is absolutely no evidence to suggest that having more money makes people any happier.

The antidote to financial worries is a financial plan. We know people worry about money.
At every level of income, people worry. In some cases, people with above average incomes suffer from above average financial stress. So let go of the myth that you'll be better off when you have more money. You will be better off when you have financial know-how and a plan.

If you currently feel uncomfortable or uneasy about money, you aren't alone. This program was designed for you and a lot of other people like you. By the end, you will feel more confident that all aspects of your personal finances (debt management, retirement, saving and investing, insurance and estate planning) are taken care of. You will be able to let go of the worries and get on with living a great life!

Taking the Worry Out of Money

If you are serious about taking charge of your finances and using money as a tool to support your life, then you need to create a plan for your finances that starts with you and what you want. While you've probably heard that it's a good idea to have a financial plan, you might be thinking, "Sure, I'll make a plan when I have money to plan." But it really works the other way around.

Having a plan that helps you articulate your goals and define your financial starting point sends a strong message that you are serious about attracting and managing the money you need to create your ideal life.

Your Money Map will help you define your financial life goals and to give you the tools, information, and structure to organize your finances to live the life you want.

- How do I balance today's goals with a secure financial future?

- Do I have enough money to retire comfortably?

- Which investments or financial products are suited to my needs?

- What do I need to know to make the best financial decisions?

Your Money Map will help you answer these questions in an organized, structured manner and will lay out the steps you need to take to get from where you are now to where you want to be.

Money Coaches Canada

Money Coaches Canada educates people to use their money to live their ideal life. Our mission is to deliver high quality financial coaching and education programs, which can be easily integrated into busy, complex and unique lives.

What We Offer

- Education and motivation

- Wisdom & experience that comes from working with thousands of people in thousands of different financial situations over the past 20 years

- Fun, succinct, practical, easy to follow, easy to implement, results-tested programs

- Understanding of the unique issues Canadians face

- Up to date facts and figures to help you make good financial decisions

- Support from a community of who, just like you, are taking financial control.

Who We Are

In 2010, Karin Mizgala and Sheila Walkington co-founded Money Coaches Canada, a national team of fee-for-service financial professionals who have a passion for helping people develop powerful and proactive relationships with their money.

Each Money Coach brings their own style and story, but we all believe in using an accessible, collaborative, plain language approach for helping clients reach their goals. We do not sell investments or financial products. Instead of earning commissions, we charge fees for our programs and services so we can provide completely independent and unbiased financial planning, coaching, education and advice to our clients.

At Money Coaches Canada, we envision a world where every Canadian has the know-how, the comfort and the confidence to use their money to live to their fullest potential. We know from our own experience that people who lead busy, complex lives need a strong financial foundation to build comfortable, balanced, and meaningful lives.

We offer one on one money coaching, workshops and educational resources.

About the Authors

Karin Mizgala, MBA, CFP With over 25 years in the financial services industry, Karin has worked as a financial planner, bank manager, investment advisor, financial educator and life skills counsellor. Karin is a Certified Financial Planner. She has an MBA from the University of Western Ontario and a BA in Psychology from York University. Karin is the CEO and co-founder of Money Coaches Canada Inc., a fee-for-service money coaching and financial planning company. She is also the co-author of UNSTUCK - *How to Get Out of Your Money Rut and Start Living the Life You Want* and a respected keynote speaker who talks about finance in a manner that inspires and motivates even those with limited financial savvy.

Sheila Walkington, BBA, CFP Sheila has a degree in Business Administration from Concordia University and is a Certified Financial Planner. She has worked in the financial sector since 1989, starting her career with Royal Trust and Vancouver Financial Planning Consultants, a branch of Assante Financial Management. In 2004, she started and built a successful fee-for-service money coaching practice to help women and couples with budgeting, getting out of debt, and planning for their future. Sheila now trains and mentors other financial professionals through Money Coaches Canada, a company she co-founded with Karin Mizgala in 2010. She is also co-author of UNSTUCK - *How to Get Out of Your Money Rut and Start Living the Life You Want*.

Your Money Map

This program will change the way you think about your money. It covers basic financial management skills and challenges you to break through your own personal financial barriers so that you can create and maintain a financial plan for your life. In this program you will:

- Explore your relationship with money

- Learn money management skills

- Clarify what you really want

- Assess where you are now

- Develop a plan to get you from where you are to where you want to be.

Our goals for this program are to:

- Educate and empower you to take control of your finances

- Illustrate how your mindset is your key to financial stability

- Transform your relationship to money into something positive, sustaining & fulfilling

- Help you develop a plan that will practically & effectively organize your finances

- Support your goals and aspirations.

Your role:

By taking this program with Money Coaches Canada you are now part of a community of people who are learning to live financially empowered lives. Enjoy the journey. Share what you are learning with others. Ask questions and make good use of the support offered to you through Money Coaches Canada (coaches, other students, helpful newsletters and web site tools), and the resources in your own community. It is up to you to do the work and take control. Your success is up to you.

What are your goals for the program?

Why did you sign up for the Your Money Map program?

_____

_____

_____

_____

How will you know if this program has helped you?

_____

_____

_____

_____

What would you like to have in place, or have accomplished, when you complete this program?

_____

_____

_____

_____

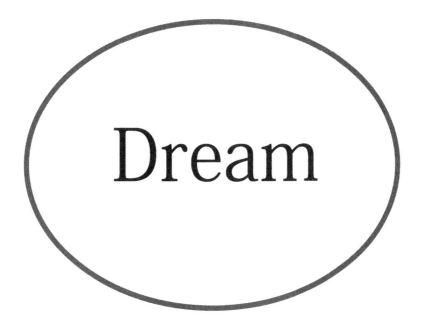

What You Really Really Want

Hint: You can't buy it but you can use your money to attain it.

The best gift you can give yourself
and those around you,
is to live your best life;
to work for happiness,
love, and peace and
to share your knowledge,
joy and compassion with others.

Does that statement seem like an odd way to start a financial planning program?
It isn't. It's essential. Your Money Map is about more than finances. It is about you, and your ability to use your money, talents, time and energy to live your best life.

Often, when people feel out of control with their finances, they avoid facing the fact that their life and their use of money are out of synch. By the time they start trying to make financial changes, they start from a place of stress or fear. That doesn't work.

Change is a radically creative process. You have to imagine doing things differently and imagine experiencing alternate outcomes. You have to be able to visualize a life that is different from the one you know. You have to see that other life so clearly that step by step you make it real.

Stress and fear close down your field of view. They might inspire you to want things to be different, but they don't help you imagine or realize new ways of being in the world. During this program we are going to challenge you to see beyond the things that have held you back. You are going to see your life the way you want it, and you are going to learn how to use your money to achieve it.

Taking control of your finances begins with awareness. And it is fundamentally supported by a brand of willfulness that stems from a positive outlook. That is very different from will power.

Will power implies that you are using energy to deny yourself something you want. That is the antithesis of this program's philosophy. Your Money Map is about using your energy and your money to get what you *really* want. It is about looking at your life and your choices in a new way.

If you are relying on will power to gain control of your finances, you are bound to struggle. The difference between an ex-smoker and a person who quits and starts every few months isn't will power. They fundamentally have different outlooks. One believes that smoking is detrimental to the quality of life they desire. The other believes smoking contributes to their quality of life. See the difference? For the person who thinks life is better with a cigarette, all the will power in the world won't make them feel good about living a healthier life - they'll only think about what they gave up. Making changes that stick means adjusting your outlook.

Throughout this program, you will have opportunities to question and re-visualize your belief systems about money. You will decide if your financial habits help you achieve the quality of life you desire. If some do, you can cultivate them with confidence. If some don't, you can change them.

At this point, all you have to do is give yourself permission to be honest with yourself about today and dream about tomorrow.

You have lived with your financial habits a long time. Even though you know intellectually and emotionally that you want to be in control of your finances, it isn't always easy to change your financial behaviours. If you try to change your actions before you change your thinking, your old patterns and habits might win out over your fledgling plan for financial control.

Open yourself to the possibility that you can use your money to live the life you want. The program will give you the tools you need to make informed decisions, imagine new ways of using your money and construct a plan that will support you through moments of doubt or indecision.

Embrace this time. Dream big. Put on your creative hat. And sharpen your pencil. You are about to see how your financial habits can contribute to you living your best life. And your plan will be your personal road map to success.

When you see it, you'll live it.

It's Your Life

Dream A Little Dream of You

You only have so much time, energy
and resources.
Why waste a second, or a penny
on things that don't matter when you can put
everything you've got
into the life you really want?

A meaningful financial plan begins with your unique goals, values and dreams. In this section, you define what is important and meaningful to you, so you can build your financial plan accordingly. Keep this clear in your mind:

Your financial plan isn't about your money, it's about your life.

The Power Behind The Plan

Dreams and goals have power. When you dream, you think creatively about the life you would like to live. When you set goals, you tell yourself and those around you that you are working towards something that is important to you. When you set goals to attain your dream life, you are saying "I'm done waiting - I'm going to make this happen."

Starting now, you are going to use your dreams and your goals to motivate you to take control of your finances. And you are going to see how keeping control of your finances will empower you to achieve the life you want.

There are a lot of people pulling at your pocket and countless pressures on your life, but when you are clear about the life you want, you are free to set your own agenda for your finances and your life.

People think that being "good with money" is about being clever with numbers. And while financially secure people do keep a close eye on their bottom line, the biggest secret to their success is that they know what they consider to be a good life and they do what they need to do to live it.

Did you know ...

Most people overspend because they don't have a compelling reason not to.

The clearer you are about the life you want to create, the less likely you'll be distracted by bright shiny objects.

20 years ago, researchers began following a group of people at the beginning of their career.

- 20% said they planned to do what they loved and worry about money later.

- 80% said they planned to work until they had enough money to quit, and then do what they really wanted to do.

Of the 1500 people in the study, 101 became millionaires.

Only 1 came from the group who waited to live their passion.

Suppressing your passion is suppressing your power.

It's not a coincidence that people who focus on living happy, fulfilling lives often end up making more *and saving more* money.

Your goals and aspirations are the greatest motivators you have to attain and maintain financial control. You might start to make changes because you don't like the way things are, but when you are tempted by your old habits, it's going to be the things you really want that motivate you to stay in control.

Are you going to plan to postpone your life, or are you going to plan to live it?

A Plan Begins With A Dream

In our culture, people think "dreamer" is a bad word. That's silly – if no one dreamt of putting down roots (literally and figuratively) we'd still be nomadic hunters and gatherers!

What's worse, people seem to enjoy using money as the prime excuse to throw cold water on a dreamer's dream. That's also silly - the way you use your money can stop you from living the life you want, or it can empower you to live the life you want. The choice is up to you.

Now here's the big question...

If money wasn't an issue, what would you aspire to do?   What future do you see?

Where would you live?   What would you be doing?   Who would you be doing it with?

Where would you work?   How much would you work?   What is the source of your joy?

What contributions would you make ?   What legacy would you leave?

This page is for your DREAMS.

Don't filter.

Don't hold back.

Nothing is silly.

Just write.

You'll "Get Real" on other pages.

Everything is permitted here.

Surprise yourself.

Keep going.

Even if you are in debt,

even if you think you can't afford it,

even if every other moment of the day you are "practical,"

write down what matters most here.

If you haven't already wondered, by now you might be saying, "What is the point of saying what I want for the future? I can't get what I need in the present!" That is the point.

Thinking about your life and your finances the way you have been hasn't given you satisfactory financial results. Seeing past your past, beyond your present, and planning for your future is how you are going to break old patterns and consciously create new ones.

When you change your mindset, you change your life.

Goals Are The Photo Ops Of Your Future

If you were to flip through the photo album of your future, each photo would mark a goal you achieved.

There you are in Tuscany. Oh, there you are moving into your first home. And look, that's the day you made your final mortgage payment. The time goes so fast.

As you build your financial plan, you will make decisions about how much to spend, save, invest, and borrow. You will learn a lot about managing your Cash Flow, investing, and talking to financial advisors. Ultimately, you will decide what is right for you based on the goals that you set for yourself. But you have to believe that you can achieve your goals.

> Desires vs. Deeds: Anna and Joel dreamt of owning their own home. They were paying a fortune to live in a small basement apartment. They had debt, and they were in the habit of getting out of town on the weekends to enjoy a better quality of life. Because she couldn't believe they would ever buy a home, Anna would buy $100 Home Lottery tickets in the hopes of getting lucky!
>
> Obstacle: They wanted a house, but they didn't let themselves want it enough to make it a priority. Instead they squandered money and perpetuated a spending pattern that made home ownership seem impossible.
>
> Moment of Clarity: Anna went through this program. She saw a house, and the stability that it would provide, as a key part of her dream life. As a goal, she wrote down that she wanted to buy a house in a year. Then she figured out what it would take to achieve the goal.
>
> Desires + Deeds: The couple stopped spending money on trips and take out. With their new consciousness about their spending, they were able to cut costs, pay off their debt and had enough money for a down payment in only 8 months!

That is the power of aligning your money with your goals. Once Anna and Joel allowed themselves to believe they could own a home, they put all their resources towards making the goal a reality.

It is entirely up to you what you do with your time, money, and energy. You can squander them and drift further from your goals or you can align your time, money and energy with your goals and let the photographer know - you are ready for your photo op!

Measurable, Achievable & True

The plain and simple truth about goals is that they have to be measurable, achievable, and heartfelt or you might as well throw your pennies in a wishing well.

Goals should be:

measurable so that you know when you've achieved them.

achievable because you will use your hunger and ability to achieve them as motivation.

true to your heart so that you are willing to stretch yourself and imagine your way past hurdles. If you aren't willing to do what it takes, you have to ask yourself if the goal is true to you.

Time and Money

Dreams are pretty abstract. Some might even call them nebulous. Goals cut dreams into bite-sized pieces. You identify an action that you can take, attach it to a time line, and figure out how much money, if any, you will need to make it happen.

Some peope find it challenging to go from the big picture to something as specific as a goal. Here's an example of how one woman turned her vision of the future into a series of goals.

Jessie is a single mom, with an average paying job and $80,000 owing on her townhouse. Ultimately, Jessie wants a master's degree, a close-knit family, a job she loves, adventures with her kids, and to not have to worry about being able to support herself or her family.

That's the dream. These are the goals she set for herself:

Goal	Cost/Value	Time Frame
1) Start a 2 year part time on-line degree	$10,000	June 2015
2) Sell my place in Vancouver	Ask $425,000	Fall 2015
3) Buy a house near my sister in Victoria	Max $410,000	Fall 2015
4) Take a leave of absence to spend time with kids and find a rewarding new job	$12,000	Summer 2017
5) Buy kayaks for the family	$5,000	Dec 2017
6) Set up RSPs for me and RESPs for the kids	$2,000 - $4,000	contribute every year

She's half way there! She knows what she wants, when she wants it, and how much she needs.

Now that Jessie is clear on her goals she can choose how she'll go about achieving them. Earn a little extra now before going back to school? Save a little extra by riding her bike to work for a year? Get the kids to do the dusting instead of the cleaning lady? Negotiate a line of credit from the bank when she buys the house in Victoria?

Goal Setting Hints

Review your dreams You wrote down your dreams so that you could visualize your best life. Now you are going to write down some goals so that you can start living it. You are identifying priorities for your money and your time so make sure you set goals that will get you what you really want.

Get debt-free You probably didn't write "debt-free" on your dream page but it was implied by all the wonderful things you could be doing with your money if it wasn't servicing your debts! If you make being debt-free a goal, you are that much closer to achieving every other goal on your page.

> **Did you know ...**
>
> opportunities to save and source money
>
> **become visible**
>
> when you are clear about what you really need the money for.

Avoid the word "next" Instead of saying, "I want to buy a house *next* year" attach a real date to the goal. Choose a month, or at least a season, and a specific year. There's always a "next", and if you aren't careful, next summer becomes next summer, which soon becomes next summer. Think about a date that feels reasonable. Write it down. Plan for it. Work towards it. Don't waffle on your goals.

Set Big Goals Stretch yourself. This is your life we are talking about. When you put your mind to it, you can find realistic ways of making your dreams come true so don't sell yourself short by setting overly conservative goals. Set at least one goal that you kind of wonder if you could achieve, but make it something you would absolutely love to do.

Be silly and serious. You need to plan to have fun. And you need to plan to replace the roof. If you have always wanted to take boxing classes - here's your chance to decide when it is going to happen. If you need to go back to school to get the job you really want, you can create a plan that will make that possible. Don't censor yourself. Whatever you want to do, you can figure it out.

Put yourself on the same page with your family. If you are in a long term relationship, or if you have dependents, your goals, like your finances, will be impacted by the significant people in your life. You need to stand up for what you believe is important for you and your family, but everyone needs to work together. If you are single with no dependents, for once you have it easier because the only person you really have to please is yourself.

It starts here. Building a financial plan is about planning to achieve your goals. So what are they? What are the photo ops of your future?

YOUR LIFE AND FINANCIAL GOALS

What do you need to do to live your dream life?

	Goal	Cost / Value	Time Frame
1.	e.g Travel - South East Asia	$10,000	Dec 2017
	_____	_____	_____
2.			
	_____	_____	_____
3.			
	_____	_____	_____
4.			
	_____	_____	_____
5.			
	_____	_____	_____
6.			
	_____	_____	_____
7.			
	_____	_____	_____
8.			
	_____	_____	_____
9.			
	_____	_____	_____

Goal are dreams with a deadline. Dreams without a deadline are just wishes.

Commitment

The C-word is a big one. Some people resist setting goals because they think, "Something might happen. I might change my mind. What if I get hit by a bus? What if I change jobs? What if I come into money? I just want to take life as it comes."

Being easy going, and free to roll with the surprises life throws at you, is a very valuable attribute. But "rolling" with change suggests that you had a specified program, something has come up, and now you are going to make adjustments. You are still committed to living your best life, you are just open to the possibility that there are new ways of achieving it.

Having a plan that is based on your goals means you have a framework. That framework will actually make it easier for you to "roll" with change. It is a support system, not a pigeon hole. And the best thing about learning how to align a financial plan with your goals is that if your goals change in the future, you'll know how to change your plan accordingly.

A very real reason that people don't commit to their goals, and their plan, is that ultimately they are afraid to change their behavior. That doesn't have to be your story. You are here to adjust your thinking, your habits and your financial behavior to suit your best life. And as that happens, you will see your commitment, and your confidence, grow.

Tell people that you are committed to your goals. Give them the opportunity to be happy for you, and support your efforts. It may feel awkward at first but tell people you trust - your spouse, friends, colleagues, then tell the clerk at the supermarket and the woman at the bus stop. People are inspired by people with conviction - and in the process of inspiring others, you will inspire yourself.

Be proactive. Stave off temptation by being honest with people about your commitment to your goals. Let them know that your life is good and that your finances are spoken for. When people understand that you are making positive changes they often want to help. If some people respond negatively to your efforts it's just because they can't see what you see. If they can't support your goals, move on. This program works, if they don't believe it, maybe they should try it!

Be positive. If you hear yourself say, "I can't" too many times you start to believe it. The whole point of gaining financial control is so that you *can* choose to do what you want with your money, and your life. The benefit of having a plan is that it will make it easier to choose to spend your money on things that support your life. And easier to choose *not* to spend your money on things that don't.

So if someone or something tempts you, instead of saying "I can't", which suggests you are denying yourself, try saying, "I'm saving for a ..." It will make a world of difference to your mindset, and to your finances.

Creative Ways to Think About Balancing Conflicting Goals

One person's conflict is another's inspiration. If you are concerned that you have goals that conflict, don't let that stop you from pursuing the goals. You just have to be creative.

Common examples of conflicting goals (by the way, everybody has them at some point)

Pay down debt AND save for retirement:

Angie and Todd are absolutely committed to paying down their debt. That is their #1 goal. But they are also committed to saving for retirement.

When they looked at their Cash Flow, it seemed they weren't earning enough to cover their basic expenses, service their loan, and contribute to an RSP on a monthly basis. Some months when they tried to do everything, they would just end up having to dip into their line of credit - and that was going against their #1 goal.

So they came up with this creative solution. On a monthly basis, they pay their expenses in full and they pay down their loan. They aren't overspending, so they aren't sliding further into debt. And every month they can watch the debt decrease, which is great motivation to carry on.

At tax time, between the two of them, they will get a $5,000 income tax refund. They will use the refund to contribute to RSPs. That not only satisfies their second goal of saving for their future, but it is a strategy they can repeat year after year.

Pay off the mortgage AND save for a holiday:

Sandra's really close to paying off her mortgage. Every month, she pays an extra $300 on her mortgage. If she keeps up these payments, she'll own her own home within 5 years! That is a huge achievement and a meaningful goal.

But she also really wants to take the family on a holiday this summer - the timing isn't great financially but it is her sister's 50th and everyone is planning a two week vacation in Spain.

Sandra knows she only has enough money to meet one of these competing goals this year, but instead of giving up on either, she uses her creativity and her motivation to live her best life.

Sticking to her goal of paying off the mortgage within 5 years is important, but it would mean so much to get the whole family together this year. So she decides to keep up the extra monthly mortgage payments, and she uses her visions of azure beaches to push herself to earn a little extra money for the holiday.

She'll use her enthusiasm to hold garage sales, pick up overtime, and take on little contracts that she can do on weekends. And when she finds the extra work tiring, she'll remind herself, it isn't forever - it's for Spain!

Start a business AND save for the future:

> Sanjit plans to open his massage therapy clinic this summer. Starting his own business is a dream come true, but it certainly puts a lot of pressure on his cash flow.
>
> In order to feel secure in his new business, he really wants to know that he has money set aside for emergencies and retirement. So contributing to his savings on a monthly basis is a goal that he is committed to.
>
> Being the savvy entrepreneur that he is, Sanjit decided to look for ways to cover some of his expenses with something other than money.
>
> Since he can't trade services for GICs, he'll use his earnings for his savings, and he'll trade services for things like setting up his web site, bookkeeping and business coaching. It isn't hard to find service providers who need massage therapy, and it is great for him to work with well-connected business people who might be able to refer business to him in the future.

Pay off student loans AND save for maternity leave:

> Kim and Brad have about $9,000 left on their student loans. They are both earning money now, but the weight of the debt has put a lot of pressure on the young couple for a number of years.
>
> They would like to pay the loans off this year, but now that Kim is pregnant, they also both want to take 6 months off work, one after the other. The baby's first year is too precious to miss.
>
> This time sensitive goal really made them take a hard look at their options.
>
> Believe it or not, they have committed to reducing their expenses and paying off the $9,000 loan before the baby is born. That means paying $1,500 per month toward the loans for the next 6 months. That's $1,000 more than they had previously paid each month.
>
> This is a great plan for balancing potentially conflicting goals for 2 reasons:
>
> > 1) By getting rid of the debt, they are removing a serious source of pressure on the family.
> >
> > 2) By cutting back their monthly living expenses for the 6 months before the baby is born, they will be prepared to live off a reduced income while they both enjoy time off with their newborn.
>
> The two are both really motivated. They've gone down to one car, they are cutting down on take out, books, clothes and all the extras that aren't nearly as important to them as starting this new phase of their life debt-free.

If you seem to have conflicting goals you might want to:

- use your tax refund, birthday money, bonuses or other windfalls to pay for one goal, and use your monthly income to pay for the other

- earn more, and use your goals to motivate you to find ways to do that

- use something other than money to achieve a goal, or part of a goal

- cut your expenses enough that you can save for both goals. Again, you'll need to believe in the goals for motivation.

- be patient. Don't pressure yourself (or your spouse) to achieve all your goals at once. Your plan should ease your burden, not add to it.

> **Did you know...**
>
> "It may be possible to have everything you really want in life, but not all at the same time." ~ Oprah Winfrey

If you have an immediate or time sensitive goal, you might simply decide to focus all your resources there.

For example, if you or your spouse is having a baby, a maternity leave isn't something you can put off. Having a nest egg may do more than support you financially, it might actually help to bring down new parent stress levels. So temporarily, you might choose to prioritize building your savings.

If you decide to temporarily put a goal on hold, set a date for when you are going to start supporting that goal again. Keep a date and cost attached to your goals - even if the date is 4 years from now!

Stay flexible and adapt, that's the key to using your goals as motivators for financial control. If you feel like you are in conflict, you'll feel pressure. And that can impair your ability to see your options.

Take the pressure off. Think creatively. Achieve your goals.

Review and Revise

You aren't carving your goals, or your financial plan, in stone. You can try them out. See how they feel. Think about them. Talk about them. If something isn't sitting right, make adjustments.

You should pull out your plan at least once a year to check in with yourself.

Acknowledge and reward your achievements.

Look back at where you were when you started - but for now, just get started!

You and Your Money

You're in this relationship for life!

The only way to profoundly improve your financial health and wealth is to understand and value both "You" and "Your Money"

Most people have very complex relationships with money. It has a powerful influence on your life: on the work you choose, your relationships, your sense of self. All reasons to build a healthy relationship.

A healthy relationship is honest, respectful and supportive.

Your money should support you to live a satisfying, fulfilling and meaningful life. In turn, you should respect your money enough to try to understand it.

You should respect yourself too. Be financially and emotionally honest with yourself. Forgive yourself and your money for past disappointments. Permit yourself and your money to grow.

If you could have a conversation with your money, what would you say?

You never let me do what I want to do.

I'm afraid I'm going to do something wrong and you'll leave me.

You embarrass me.

I don't know where you are half the time!

You are holding me back.

Or

You and I are growing together.

You are always there when I need you.

I trust that if I take care of you, you'll take care of me.

You help me be the person I really want to be.

What would your money say to you?

You take me for granted.

You just throw me away when your friends come around.

You don't take me seriously.

You only pay attention to me when you want something.

You don't understand me.

Or

I'm here for you.

You and I are growing together.

We take good care of each other.

We can build a dream life together.

What do you think? Do you and your money need a little relationship counselling? Do you feel the trust? The appreciation? The understanding?

Ok, money doesn't really have feelings. But you do. Understanding how your financial emotions impact your financial decisions is key to breaking unconscious patterns and unlocking your financial power.

Uncovering the Unconscious: Unmixing the Mixed Messages

The first step is to understand where your emotions, assumptions and baggage come from. Just like your relationships with people, your relationship with money is heavily influenced by those around you.

We learn by observing. We observe our parents, our peers, the media. Unfortunately, they aren't always great teachers and they rarely compare notes so the messages we get about money get ridiculously mixed up. It is up to you to turn off the noise and check in with yourself. This is where you discover something about what matters to the *You* in the *You and Your Money* relationship.

Mixed Message #1: Do as I say, not as I do.

Yeah, that worked. Your parents may or may not have intentionally taught you about money, but without a doubt you learned a lot from them. Whatever you experienced in your family, good and bad, set the stage for the way you relate to money today.

This story illustrates how parents can inadvertently send their children very different messages:

The lessons Amy learned from her father were very direct:

"My first allowance was 5 pennies. One penny had to go to helping someone else and the other four were for me. Every Sunday, when Dad gave me my allowance I had to account for what I had done with the previous week's pennies.

He taught me to use my money to help others and to help myself and he taught me to plan for the future – he had me investing in RSPs and doing my own taxes when I was 18!"

The lessons Amy learned from her mother were indirect:

"My mother used money as an excuse for not taking control of her life. She used to say, "If I had the money, I would leave your father, get my own apartment and travel." Like many people of her generation, she felt powerless in her marriage. I spent my teenage years trying to prove that she had the power to change her life, but her argument against me often came back to money. I learned that I never wanted to feel powerless, and that maintaining financial control of my life would afford me precious choices."

Good and Bad, what did your family teach you about money?

Bring your memories to a level of awareness where you can look at the choices you are making today, and assess if you truly own your actions or if you are reacting to a past that you need to lay to rest.

This page is for discovering how your past impacts your present.

Maybe you had great role models but struggle to apply their lessons to your modern life.

Maybe you adopted dysfunctional behaviors and beliefs.

You might try to do the opposite of what you saw.

Maybe you spend recklessly to counteract the penny pinching you grew up hating.

Maybe you are very protective of your money because you watched others get taken advantage of.

Be honest with yourself here.

Here's the good news. You can use your discoveries to move forward and you can use your money to live the life you want. You are an adult. You can change your habits if you want. And if you are a parent, you can teach your children to manage their money wisely. Pass on confidence to the next generation, instead of confusion.

Mixed Message #2 Money can't buy happiness, but buying stuff is fun and makes you feel better.

The first part of the message is true. Money can't buy happiness.

Research by the University of Pennsylvania suggests that happiness is related to your feelings of community engagement, the alignment of your actions and your goals, living and working from your strengths, and believe it or not – practice. (Working an extra smile into your day will give you more of a boost than an energy drink!)

So what about the second part of the message. Does buying stuff make you feel better? Is it fun?

Advertising campaigns, and even friends reinforce the pleasures of parting with your hard earned cash. They tell you that, "You'll be happier, safer, healthier, thinner (fill in your fear here) when you have…".

But picture it, you've bought all the right anti-aging, soul-enlightening, nonfat, memory-boosting, fast-acting, self-cleaning, make-more-time-for-yourself stuff you can afford (and possibly a bit more). Now you are looking at your bank statement; a print out of all the fun you've had. Are you still having fun?

> According to the Oxford English Dictionary:
>
> Fun, n. . A cheat or trick; a hoax, a practical joke. Diversion, amusement, sport; also, boisterous jocularity or gaiety, drollery. Also, a source or cause of amusement or pleasure. Often used ironically.

Buying stuff to make yourself feel better is certainly a diversion tactic. But if you think the amusement you get out of it is lasting, you are tricking yourself.

See if you recognize this cycle of fun: I'm stressed. I need to have some fun. I buy things and go places that cost a bit more than I can really afford but, I'm worth it. I eventually get my credit card statement. I see just how much fun I had. I'm stressed.

Our culture touts fun as the antidote to stress and unhappiness. But when fun comes back to cause you stress, you need to find a new source of amusement and think about what truly brings you pleasure.

The real antidote to stress is a positive outlook and a plan!

Mixed Message #3 Do more. Buy more. Earn more. Relax more. Huh?

It is easy to see why we need to relax, but who can? If you sit still for a moment, it's time you could be doing, buying, experiencing or working. The solution seems to be to do all those things while you relax! What happened to laying down on a lawn chair, or walking in the park? Now we chill out at the mall! Or by spending $120 on a massage and manicure. Or by spending $2,500 on an all-inclusive week in Cancun and don't forget to cram two weeks of work into one before you go! Ahhh.

Shopping, spa treatments and holidays are great (really great) but if you have to spend more than you earn to relax you are going to stress yourself out! It is basic math:

Working your tail off + debt = stress

Do you ever wonder if our culture's new found passion for expensive relaxation is really just a cover for a communal panic caused by living beyond our means?

So let go of the myth that *more is more*. Most of us don't really need more but we are conditioned to want more, consume more, and expect more.

When architects and designers design a room for relaxation they work with the *less is more* philosophy. Lose the clutter. Turn off the noise. Take the pressure off. Enjoy living within your means.

Mixed Message # 4 You deserve it.

Deserve what? Do you deserve to be in debt? Do you deserve to be panicked about money? Do you deserve to be a slave to a pay cheque? Think about that the next time you want to "treat" yourself to something you think you deserve but know you can't afford.

You deserve to live your best life. You deserve to feel satisfaction and contentment when you pick up your bank statement. You deserve to achieve your goals. You deserve financial control of your life!

Mixed Message # 5 We're friends, we can talk about anything, except money.

Why is it that when friends get together we will share the most intimate details of our sex lives but we won't talk about money? Your friends can teach you how to trick your partner into thinking it was his idea to renovate the kitchen, but who's sharing secrets about their RSP investments?

Break the silence. We can learn and share and shed financial chains together. Talk to your friends about what you learn in this program. Inquire after their financial health. Let them know they can talk to you about their hopes and fears. Build a support network of people who are financially empowered.

Take a minute to describe your current relationship with your money.

What would it mean to you to have control of your money?
What does it mean to you to not have control of your money?
What emotions do you associate with money? Fear? Shame? Frustration? Joy?

What does money mean to you?

Security
Power
Acceptance
Love
Freedom
Happiness

What else?

Blocks to Financial Success

Is your relationship to money standing between you and your goals?

"Your present circumstances
don't determine where you can go,
they merely determine
where you start."

~Nido Qubein

You are going to have to take control. You know that. On some level you are probably excited about it, and on some level you are probably worried about what you might have to face.

Be assured of this. Living the life you want may take some getting used to, but it isn't scary. Being alone at 65 with no savings and no house is scary. Living without financial control is scary. It's also stressful, painful and self-destructive. Anything you encounter facing your financial facts will pale in comparison. What's better, any fears you face now are just obstacles to overcome.

Still, it is important to know that you will experience obstacles. You will wonder if you're doing the right thing or if you can even do this. You can. And it is normal to wonder - you are learning new habits and ways to think about money.

You want to reach your goals. You are going down a new financial path. Your financial plan is your road map. It will help you navigate. If at a certain point you wonder if you have taken a wrong turn, or if the road seems too long, side step your worries. Pull out the plan.

Maybe you'll see a new way around an obstacle. Or maybe you'll realize that you are exactly where you're supposed to be.

Obstacles You Can Overcome

This is a list of the most common obstacles people encounter en route to financial control. It's here to help you recognize obstacles when you see them.

Get familiar with these challenges, when one pops out of the bushes, don't turn back. Consult your plan. Consult other financially empowered people. Give yourself permission to imagine a way to your goals. If you recognize some of these already, you are not alone.

What if syndrome What if it's worse than I thought? What if I'm miserable? What if I can't?

Abdicating responsibility Someone else can probably manage things better than I can.

Intimidation I'd be embarrassed to ask questions, everyone knows more than I do.

Mommy & Daddy syndrome My parents will leave me money. My Dad will always bail me out.

Shame I should have done things differently, I should be further ahead than I am.

Conflicts with spouse If we can't agree I'd rather drop it. It's easier not to talk about it.

I wish syndrome I wish I could win the lottery or get an inheritance from a long lost uncle.

Procrastination I don't have enough money yet, I'll do this when I have more.

Prince Charming syndrome My husband or husband-to-be will take care of me.

Conflicted values I shouldn't focus on money, that's what selfish people do.

Lack of time I don't have time to cook, let alone figure out how much I spend on take out.

Lack of interest I have better things to do with my time.

Lack of forgiveness I've made so many financial mistakes, I can't do this.

Lack of support I don't know where to turn for help.

Lack of confidence It's too complicated, I'll never get this right. I don't know where to start.

Here's what you need to know about these (and other) obstacles, they pretty much all come back to fear. And fear always tries to steer you back to the path it knows. Fear can make you really uncomfortable and try to trick you into thinking your old habits were more conducive to the good life. Were they? Are you living the good life? Don't you want things to change?

To stay on course, take a good look at the obstacle that is in your way. Step away from it. Shine a light on it. See it for what it is. A belief? A learned behavior? A value judgement? Something from a past or present relationship? Whatever it is, don't let it hold you back anymore. Imagine a way through.

If you abdicate responsibility or put your head in the sand financially you will lose your choices, your money and your freedom. You have absolutely nothing to lose by taking control of your finances.

Karin's Life Transition Story

When I graduated from university, I was immediately invited into the corporate fast track. I lived in Toronto. I worked on Bay Street. I spent money on clothes, fine dining and exotic vacations. Still, I found myself frustrated and disillusioned. Like many, I blamed Toronto and I moved to Vancouver.

It took some getting used to, but I soon embraced the Vancouver lifestyle: yoga, meditation and a journey in self-exploration. My heart and soul were crying out for something more than the "make it bigger, stronger, faster" mantra of the corporate world.

During this transition, I didn't dismiss my finances, in fact, it was quite the opposite. It become more important than ever for me to take a good hard look at my relationship to money and deal head-on with how I managed my Cash Flow.

Because my goals and my focus had changed, it was clear that I couldn't continue to spend the way I had been. Before I started The Women's Financial Learning Centre and Money Coaches Canada, I paid off my debts and created a Spending and Savings Plan that would support me to start my businesses and live a fulfilling life.

I admit to thinking the changes would be difficult. But when I looked at my spending patterns and used the filter of what was truly important to me, it wasn't hard to cut out the frills.

I now take out a certain amount of cash each week for my discretionary expenses and if I don't have the cash for something, I don't buy it. Simple as that. And the good news is that I'm no longer falling into the, "I deserve to have this" or the, "I'm feeling stressed so I'll buy something to feel better" spending traps. I noticed that the better I felt about how I was living my life, the less I wanted/needed to spend.

Ignore the voice of doom whether it's yours or someone else's. Just remember that taking control of your finances isn't impossible. It isn't even painful. It is surprisingly exciting!

Jessica and her partner built their plan together. She said, "I get excited thinking about my lack of stress. I was worried about being destitute and living in a hovel. Now I think, our future is good. If we stick to the plan we can have a holiday every year. And what's so exciting is that cutting back hasn't been painful at all! I'm just careful, and I find new ways of saving money all the time."

Julie said "Doing the work hasn't stressed me out at all. It was **not** doing the work that was really stressing me out."

Here's what you need to remember:

Taking charge of your finances isn't about limiting yourself or judging yourself.

It is about educating, enlightening and empowering yourself to have the life you want.

The only thing you are depriving yourself of is stress and poverty.

You can do this. You have support.

Claiming Your Financial Power

Take small, manageable steps towards financial empowerment and be realistic with what you can accomplish at any one time. There's no need to be an expert overnight. If you try to absorb too much new information or take on too many tasks on your financial to-do list, you're more likely to be overwhelmed and abandon your best intentions altogether.

Also, remember the road to financial enlightenment is a process and it's easy enough to fall back into negative patterns. Change doesn't always happen immediately so be patient and acknowledge all wins no matter how small they may be. Cross your financial to-do's off your list with delight, savour the joy of having the money in your account before your vacation, and burn your mortgage statements when the house is paid off.

Just Do Your Best

That's all you have to do. If you get confused, ask questions. If you think you can't do something, give yourself an extra minute, hour, day to think through your options and take conscious action.

You know what you want. You have some ideas about the obstacles that have stopped you before. Now you are ready to narrow your focus and put a plan in place.

You are about to build a bridge between possibilities and practicalities.

To be really effective, it's hard to focus on more than two or three goals at a time.

On the next page, list the top 2 or 3 goals you would like to focus on. Give them a dollar value and a time frame. Then think about what obstacles might get between you and your goals. What action steps can you take to move you closer to your goals or navigate around the obstacles?

Top 3 Goals!

- Are your goals clear & measurable with a time frame?
- What obstacles might hinder achieving your goal?
- What action steps will you take to achieve the goal, or overcome the obstacles?

Obstacles

Action Steps

1. Goal: _____

   Dollar Value: _____

   Time Frame: _____

2. Goal: _____

   Dollar Value: _____

   Time Frame: _____

3. Goal: _____

   Dollar Value: _____

   Time Frame: _____

"It takes as much energy to wish as it does to plan."

- Eleanor Roosevelt

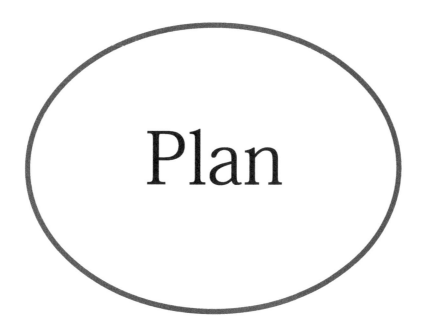

38

Your Financial Starting Point

"I am indeed rich,
since my income is superior to my expense,
and my expense
is equal to my wishes."

~Kahlil Gibran

Give Yourself The Freedom to Choose

Spending money isn't bad. Debt isn't even necessarily bad. But as anyone who has ever seen a single digit bank account knows, no money and no plan means no choices.

To gain and maintain financial control you need to understand how your money comes in and how it goes out.

It is about awareness. And with awareness comes freedom.

This section will help you build your awareness about your current financial situation. It is also an opportunity to reflect on whether or not your spending is in line with your values. By the end, you will know your current Net Worth, your current Cash Flow and you will have a Spending and Savings Plan that will help you to make financial decisions that work for you. This is where you really start taking control!

Net Worth

Net Worth is a financial snapshot of where you stand at one point in time. It is the difference between what you *own* and what you *owe*.

Assets (What You Own) − **Liabilities** (What You Owe) = **Net Worth**

Common examples of Assets: house, car, cash, antique collection, RSPs and pension savings

Common examples of Liabilities: student loan, credit card debt, mortgage, line of credit

---

Your Net Worth can be improved by decreasing debt, committing more money to your investments, earning a greater rate of return on your investments, or enjoying an increase in the value of your assets (for example, an increase in the value of your home will improve your Net Worth).

Uses of Net Worth

- to track your progress year to year - it is a quick indication of forward and backward motion

- to apply for a bank loan or mortgage - lenders need to see your whole financial picture

- to draw up your will and for estate planning

Instructions for Completing a Net Worth Statement

Start by filling in the details of your current financial picture.

In the Details For Your Net Worth Statement worksheet, write down all the things you own: house, car, RSPs, stocks, bonds, cash accounts, etc.

Include the financial institution your RSPs or savings are with, and any additional details, such as the year and model of your car, the current price of the stocks you own and their original price, etc. All these details add colour to your financial snapshot.

Then list your debts and the amounts owing: your mortgage, line of credit, student loans, credit cards, personal loans, family loans, outstanding bills, etc.

Make note of who the lender is, how much you are repaying per week, per month or per year, what the interest rate is, and, for credit cards and lines of credit, what your credit limit is.

Use the boxes on the details page to total your assets and liabilities. Then carry the totals forward to the Net Worth Statement worksheet on the next page. Then, tally everything up to see your Net Worth.

DETAILS FOR YOUR NET WORTH STATEMENT

Current Date:

1. CASH & DEPOSIT ACCOUNTS   **Amount** | $0 |
  Chequing _____
  Savings _____
  Other _____
  Other _____

2. OUTSTANDING DEBT   **Financial Institution**   **Amount** | $0 |
  Credit Card #1 _____   _____
  Credit Card #2 _____   _____
  Loan _____   _____
  Line of Credit _____   _____
  Car Loan _____   _____
  Home Buyer's Plan _____   _____

3. RSP's | $0 |

  Financial Institution   **Amount**
  _____   _____
  _____   _____
  _____   _____

4. NON - RSP INVESTMENTS | $0 |
  (eg. GICs, CSBs, Stocks, Employee Share Purchase Plan, Mutual Funds)

  Financial Institution   **Amount**
  _____   _____
  _____   _____
  _____   _____

5. PRINCIPAL RESIDENCE   *Current Value of Home:* | ____ |
  Mortgage Company _____   *Mortgage Balance:* | ____ |
  Interest Rate _____
  Mortgage Payment _____
  Frequency of Payment _____
  Maturity Date _____

6. VEHICLE(S)   **Type**   **Current Value** | $0 |
  Vehicle #1 _____   _____
  Vehicle #2 _____   _____

7. PENSION - DEFINED CONTRIBUTION   *Current Value:* | ____ |

8. OTHER | ____ |

© Money Coaches Canada 2014

NET WORTH STATEMENT

Current Date:

	ASSETS	LIABILITIES
INVESTMENT ASSETS AND LIABILITIES		
CASH & DEPOSIT ACCOUNTS	0	0
OUTSTANDING DEBT	0	0
RSPs	0	0
NON - RSP INVESTMENTS	0	0
OTHER:		
OTHER:		
Total Investment Assets and Liabilities:	$ -	$ -
LONG-TERM ASSETS AND LIABILITIES		
PRINCIPAL RESIDENCE	0	0
VEHICLE(S)	0	0
PENSION - DEFINED CONTRIBUTION	0	0
OTHER:	0	0
OTHER:		
Total Long-Term Assets & Liabilities:	$ -	$ -
TOTAL ASSETS AND LIABILITIES	$ -	$ -
NET WORTH (Assets - Liabilities)		$ -

How does it feel to see your Net Worth?

_____

_____

_____

Cash Flow

Cash Flow looks at how money flows into your household (e.g. income, bonuses, tax refunds, or government benefits, etc.) and how it flows out (spending, saving, bills, charity, etc.).

This is often the most dreaded part of money management. But it is important and it isn't hard, really. So, don't put it off. If you put it off, you put off attaining financial control. You can do this.

Successfully managing Cash Flow is your key to financial control.

Tracking your savings and spending (and being aware of your own personal patterns) will give you an awareness that has more long term value than anything you can invest in, buy or sell.

> The most important, and most overlooked financial concept is this:
>
> ### spend less than you earn.

Shocking, right? And yet, according to Statistics Canada, nearly half of Canadian households currently spend more than they earn. No wonder people are stressed about money!

If you understand clearly what money is coming in and what's going out, then you are in a position to make informed, conscious decisions about your money and your life. You can use your money to build the life you want instead of building the debt and financial insecurity you don't.

The Cash Flow worksheet will help you analyze your current income, as well as your spending and savings patterns, and identify expenses you can trim to free up more money for your goals.

Try not to worry about what you are going to find out. Just fill in the boxes. If it turns out that you spend more than you earn, you'll find a way to reduce your expenses or make more money. And you'll put it in your plan.

> Laura knew she was sinking but she was afraid to face it. When she did her Cash Flow, she saw in black and white that every month she was spending $1,000 more than she was earning.
>
> If she had kept her head in the sand, each year would have sunk her another $12,000 in debt.
>
> Laura had to face facts. She could either cut her expenses or earn more money. She liked the life she was building, so instead of cutting back she was inspired to earn more.
>
> The next month she landed a great job that increased her salary by $30,000! After taxes, she took home $18,000 more per year - more than she needed to live the life she loved.
>
> Doing a Cash Flow didn't make Laura any more capable of getting the higher paying job. The information, coupled with the desire to live the life she wanted, was a powerful motivator.
>
> What's scary is that her fear of facing the numbers could have cost her $12,000 a year in debt and $18,000 in lost revenue!

Instructions for Completing the Cash Flow Worksheet

You'll need to collect a few things to get started.

Pull out the last three months of bank and credit card statements. These will give you an itemized list of your spending. (If you use cash, estimate your expenses. Then, keep your receipts for the next month and go back over your estimates to confirm.)

Review your statements. You want to look at all three months so that you can get an average of what you have been spending on clothes, food, gas, eating out, etc.

There are always irregularities. You will use the last three months of information to estimate your expenses. You may need to make adjustments if the months you've tracked are out of the ordinary.

You will also need some recent pay cheque stubs. Find your *net income* (the amount you take home).

If you get paid every two weeks, we recommend you use the amount you take home over two pay cheques as your monthly income. There will be two months a year when you receive an extra pay cheque. Make a note of that - if you plan to live off of two pay cheques a month, you'll be able to use those extra pay-days to boost your savings or pay down debt!

If your employer deducts RSP contributions, charitable donations or anything over and above the usual tax deductions, make a note of that too. Those expenses don't need to be shown on your Cash Flow because you have already accounted for them by using your net income as a starting point.

If you are self-employed or work on commission, determining a monthly income can be a challenge. We suggest that you try paying yourself a "regular salary" every month. What is a reasonable amount of money that you can count on? Use the minimum amount for planning purposes. This way you know you can live on the minimum and any extra can go toward building up a buffer for slow times, holidays or an investment in your business.

Now you can get going on filling in your Cash Flow.

Start by filling out your regular monthly income and then do some easy things like regular monthly expenses (rent or mortgage payments) – this will get the momentum going!

Then plunk in some average expenses. What did the last three months of spending tell you? What was your average grocery bill for the month? Clothes? Gas?

Next, think about expenses that only come up a few times a year, such as car repairs, gifts, and travel. Estimate a total for those expenses, divide it by 12, and put that figure in the monthly column. You may not pay the bills in 12 monthly installments but imagine you are setting money aside each month so that you have the total amount when the bill comes due. You might find that you start doing that!

Note: If you need to call anyone for information, for example your investment advisor, benefits advisor at work, or creditors, make a list of the names and phone numbers so that you have them handy.

YOUR CASH FLOW

	Monthly	Annual
NET INCOME		
Income - Me (after tax and deductions)		
Income - Spouse (after tax and deductions)		
Government Benefits		
Other		
TOTAL NET INCOME	$	$
EXPENSES:		
Fixed Costs & Regular Monthly Payments		
Rent / Mortgage		
Strata fees		
Property Insurance (if paid monthly)		
Property Taxes (if paid monthly)		
Heat/Gas		
Hydro		
Phone		
Cable		
Internet		
Cell Phone(s)		
Childcare / Allowance / Children's Expenses		
Life or Disability Insurance Premiums		
Provincial Health Premiums (ie MSP, OHIP)		
Car payment		
RSP		
RESP		
Non-RSP Savings		
Bank Fees		
Car Insurance (if paid monthly)		
Charitable Donation (if paid monthly)		
Monthly Payment Credit Card # 1 (if cards paid off monthly, put $0)		
Monthly Payment Credit Card # 2 (if cards paid off monthly, put $0)		
Loan Payment		
Line of Credit Payment		
Other		
Other		
Other		
Total Fixed Costs and Regular Monthly Payments	$	$
Monthly Expenses		
Groceries		
Pet food and treats		
Personal Care (hair cuts, dry cleaning, pharmacy)		
Gas		
Taxis / Bus/ Parking		
Snacks, Lunches at work, Coffees		
Entertainment (Dining out, movies, etc)		
Alcohol (beer/wine) or Cigarettes		
Other		
Total Monthly Expenses	$	$
Lump Sum and Annual Expenses		
Property Taxes (if paid annually)		
Property Insurance (if paid annually)		
Home Repairs and Maintenance		
Car Repairs and Maintenance		
Car Insurance (if paid annually)		
Medical & Dental		
Clothing		
Gifts - Birthdays, Christmas, other		
Charitable Donations (if paid annually)		
Hobbies and/or Children's Activities		
Self-Improvement		
Clubs & Memberships		
Professional / Accounting Fees		
Vet		
Computer/Electronics supplies and equipment		
Travel & Vacations		
Other		
Total Lump Sum and Annual Expenses	$	$
TOTAL EXPENSES	$	$
CASH FLOW SURPLUS (DEFICIT):	$	$

Interpreting the Numbers

Preparing a Cash Flow can be an eye-opening experience. You might be surprised to see how well you are already doing. Or you might see that you've left yourself considerable room for improvement.

Either way, you can also see how your spending habits line up with your goals. If you see that more money flows out to the cable company than to your RSPs, you might want to ask yourself if Seinfeld will foot the bill for your retirement home.

In reviewing your worksheet, here are some serious questions to ask yourself:

Are you spending more than you earn?

Are you spending or allocating enough money for your goals?

Does it show that there's money left over at the end of the month when you know there isn't? (If so, what did you forget to include? Do you make two loan payments a month and only account for one? Did you include car insurance? Gifts? Clothes? Travel?)

Does your spending reflect your values and what's important to you?

Are you saving enough to see you through an emergency?

Are you saving for retirement?

Do you want to make some changes? (There's another sheet for that coming up!)

Once you have an accurate picture of your current incomings and out goings, you will be surprised by how easy it is to find ways to make simple changes that have massive impacts.

This is where the magic begins!

Turning The Numbers Into Conscious Choices

There are a lot of things you have to spend money on. Take the financial pressure off by having a plan that reflects your financial realities and your financial goals.

Review your goals to remind yourself what really matters to you. And be real. If doing your Cash Flow has reminded you of goals or values that you didn't write down before, go back and add them now.

Maybe seeing how much you have been spending on renovations helped you realize that a "beautiful and secure home" is a big part of your best life. If so, write it down as a goal and set an annual dollar value for renovations on your goals sheet (you might need to update your Top 3 Goals sheet too). If on the other hand you hate that you spend more on faucets than on a goal that really matters to you, it will be easier for you to choose to spend less at the home improvement store from now on.

Review your expenses line by line. Have a good look at where you're spending your money and ask yourself: is this expense necessary? Could I do better? Is it really important to me? Likely, you will be surprised by how much you are spending in some categories without even noticing.

Review your income. Is it time to ask for the raise they've been hinting about? Is there a way to bring in some additional income through overtime, a part time job, renting out a room in your house?

Now watch yourself spend money. Every time you spend, ask yourself: am I moving one step closer to my goal? Or one step further away? Do I really want this? Or do I want something else more?

You deserve to live your best life. When you see ways to achieve your goals, you will inevitably start to see your spending decrease and your savings for your goals will increase. The answer to "how" will become obvious because you'll be motivated by your goals.

Sheila and David have travel as a top priority goal.

Every month we set aside $300 for a big trip - this year it was the Arizona desert, next year it's Italy - and another $100 for short jaunts to Whistler, and trips to visit family out East.

Recently we realized that if we could just find another $60 a month, we could squeeze in a whole extra trip each year. We reviewed our Cash Flow, looking for something that we could cut by $60. It didn't take long to spot that was exactly what we were paying our cleaner.

David and I will quite happily take turns vacuuming to get an extra weekend away!

Consciously Create a Spending and Savings Plan

This is where you really start thinking creatively. Your Spending and Savings Plan is like a target Cash Flow.

If you can't afford your goals *and* your lifestyle in your current Cash Flow, you need to make some changes and your Spending and Savings Plan will function as a guide to help you use your money to your best advantage.

To start your Spending and Savings Plan you need to know:

- how much income you earn after taxes and deductions (see current Cash Flow worksheet)

- how much money you spend on your current lifestyle (see current Cash Flow worksheet)

- how much you need for your goals (see Goals worksheet)

Then you need to open yourself up to seeing what financial changes you can make, so that you can start living the life you want with the money you have. What would better reflect your goals and values? What changes would free up money for the things that matter? What would it take to gain control?

Instructions for Completing the Spending and Savings Plan

Use the next worksheet to start your Spending and Savings Plan. Some lines you will just copy over from your Cash Flow worksheet (e.g. unless you plan to move, you aren't going to reduce your property tax).

For expenses from the Cash Flow worksheet that you want to change, fill in a projected number for what you would like to spend.

Use your instincts to guide you, and for a little extra guidance, use the hints on the next page.

You will likely go over this a few times before you settle on numbers that work for you, so use pencil, stay open, and start your plan.

Hints on Setting Reasonable Targets

Plan to spend less than you earn. Keep that basic principle in mind as you create your plan. If you are currently overspending every month, start by looking for ways to cut back. If you can imagine spending less on gasoline and parking by car pooling, make that part of your plan - write it down.

Plan for your goals. If you have a goal to start art classes, use a Savings Goal line and fill in the amount you need to set aside each month to reach your goal. If you also have a goal to buy a condo and you need to save for a down payment, use the next Savings Goal line for the house. Your goals are central to your plan; you have to eat but you also have to have money for your goals. This is where you start to think about how you can make that happen.

Plan to have fun. Your financial plan won't work if you feel too constrained. The point is to free up money for the things that matter and sometimes going out with your friends matters - so don't forget to allocate some money for fun.

And don't feel guilty about spending this money - enjoy it - it's just as much a part of your plan, and just as important, as paying down debt. The key is to really enjoy spending the money you have allocated, and not to spend a penny more.

Plan to give a little to get a little. Say you want to increase your savings by $50 a month. That money has to come from somewhere. As you write it down on your plan, decide what area you can shave by $50 and make that change on your plan as well. Can you car pool and share parking costs? Can you be more careful at the grocery store and cut back that monthly expense? Thinking in terms of give and take will help you write the plan, and it will also help you stick to it.

Plan to stop worrying. If you create a Spending and Savings Plan that covers your needs and your goals, you will know exactly how much money you have to spend on things. So what's to worry about? You will know how much you can spend on hair cuts and you will have decided that it's okay. You will know how much you are saving for retirement and that you are on track. You will know that you have budgeted for car repairs and debt repayment and that one doesn't have to preclude the other.

Plan so that choices are easy. If your brother asks you to join him for a ski weekend, you won't have to worry about whether or not you can afford it. If you have a travel line, you will know what you planned to spend on travel and you will know what you can afford. Better still, if it is a smidgen over budget, and it is important to you, you will know how to go back over the plan and choose something to cut back on to free up some cash. And if it isn't in the plan, you can tell him that it isn't in your plan. Full stop. It's your money - your life!

Plan to have more breathing room in the future. All things in good time. If things are tight now, don't despair. Be creative about increasing your income so that you can expand your spending and savings in the future. If you plan for it, you can have room to maneuver .

SPENDING AND SAVINGS PLAN

NET INCOME

	Monthly	Annual	Changes
Income - Me (after tax and deductions)			
Income - Spouse (after tax and deductions)			
Bonus/Overtime			
Government Benefits			
Rental Income			
Other			
TOTAL NET INCOME			

EXPENSES:

MAIN CHEQUING - Monthly Fixed Costs

	Monthly	Annual	Changes
Rent / Mortgage			
Condo/Strata Fees			
Property Insurance (if paid monthly)			
Property Taxes (if paid monthly)			
Gas or Oil (for heating)			
Hydro			
Phone			
Cable			
Internet			
Cell Phone(s)			
House Alarm			
Childcare / Allowance / Children's Expenses			
Life Insurance Premiums			
Disability Insurance Premiums			
Health Premiums			
Vehicle Payments			
RSP			
RESPs			
Non-RSP Savings			
Bank Fees			
Vehicle Insurance (if paid monthly)			
Charitable Donation			
Clubs or Gym Membership (if paid monthly)			
Credit Card #1 Pymt			
Credit Card #2 Pymt			
Personal Loan / Student Loan Payment			
Line of Credit Payment			
Other			
Total Monthly Fixed Costs			

MONTHLY SPENDING - Chequing #2

	Monthly	Annual	Changes
Groceries & Cleaning Supplies			
Pet Food and Treats			
Pharmacy, Toiletries			
Gas for Vehicle			
Taxis / Bus/ Parking			
Snacks and Lunches at work			
Entertainment - Dining out, Movies, etc.			
Alcohol - (beer/wine) and/or Cigarettes			
Other			
Total Monthly Spending			

SAVINGS ACCOUNTS - Lump Sum and Annual Expenses

	Monthly	Annual	Changes
Fixed Annual & Lump Sum Expenses			
Property Taxes (if paid annually)			
Vehicle Insurance (if paid annually)			
Property Insurance (if paid annually)			
Clubs or Memberships (if paid annually)			
Magazine Subscriptions			
Costco Membership/Credit Card Annual Fees			
Professional / Accounting Fees			
Variable Annual & Lump Sum Expenses			
Home Repairs, Furniture and Household Items			
Vehicle Repairs and Maintenance			
Medical, Dental, Glasses, Contacts			
Personal Care (hair care, cosmetics, dry cleaning)			
Clothing, Shoes, Outerwear			
Gifts and Donations			
Children's Activities			
Vet Bills			
Travel, Vacations and Family Fun			
Self-Improvement & Hobbies			
Computer/Electronics			
Holiday Pay (if self-employed)			
Other			
Total Lump Sum and Annual Expenses			
TOTAL EXPENSES			

	Monthly	Annual	Changes
CASH FLOW SURPLUS (DEFICIT):			

Even Changes Can Change

Now you have a Spending and Savings Plan that reflects your values. That doesn't mean it's perfect.

You will continually need to fine tune your choices to create a balance between living the lifestyle you want today and the one you are planning for your future.

You might find that the amount of money you thought you needed, and the amount you actually need for things changes. So make adjustments. Just make sure that when you make changes, you stay on program.

Sheila knows her spending and savings habits very well.

I know that if I have cash in my pocket, I'm likely to spend it. But I'm also a firm believer that having a little "guilt-free" money helps people stay on program with their spending. It's great to treat yourself... in healthy ways.

I initially put $100 a week into my Spending and Savings Plan for guilt-free treats (lattes, lunches out, nail polish etc).

But I soon realized it was more than I really needed. Some weeks I had money left over at the end of the week, and other weeks I felt I was just being frivolous by going out for lunch more often than I needed.

So, I cut my "guilt-free" cash in half and put the balance in my travel savings. I still get treats and I get more travel. Now that's living!

Sheila's been helping people with her finances for over 20 years and she still learns, and makes adjustments. You will too.

Ideally, you will review your Net Worth annually and your Spending and Savings Plan periodically throughout the year. Challenge yourself - if you are consistently overspending in one area ask yourself if you need to change your plan or your behaviour ... or both. If you are consistently underspending, ask yourself the same questions. This will empower you to make choices *and changes* with confidence.

On Track Money Management System

Annual income twenty pounds, annual expenditure nineteen pounds nineteen and six, result happiness. Annual income twenty pounds, annual expenditure twenty pounds ought and six, result misery.

~Charles Dickens

Once you've completed your Spending and Savings Plan worksheet so that, at least on paper, you're living within your means and saving for your goals, you need to make sure you can stick with the program.

Budget Blues

We're often asked about the best accounting or budgeting software to keep track of expenses, such as Quicken or Microsoft Money. Honestly, we're not big fans of any budgeting software.

The trouble is most people don't use their 'money time' wisely - and often focus their attention on the wrong things when it comes to budgeting programs. Staying on track with your money isn't about dumping a whole bunch of numbers into a computer every month and then wasting time juggling those figures. There's a feeling that if you put them all neatly on a spreadsheet, somehow magically the numbers will balance and at the end of the month you won't have spent more than you made.

The key is to do something useful with the information you've been gathering so diligently about your spending and to figure out what the numbers mean.

Added to that is the fact that the word 'budget' has such negative connotations. It feels restrictive as if somebody is slapping you on the wrist; it's like you can never have any fun. Faced with that prospect, it's no wonder people aren't motivated to live on a budget.

The real purpose for knowing how much you are spending is to make sure you're living within your means and to help you plan spending for the year ahead. You also need to know if you are setting enough money aside for important life goals — travel, retirement, children's education, charity or making a difference in the world.

If you are living within your means and working towards your goals, then you can monitor your budget by looking at the pace of your debt reduction, the quality of your life on a day-to-day basis and your progress in reaching your goals. Your system is working and you may not need to change it.

However, if you're running up balances on your credit card or line of credit, re-mortgaging your home or never making headway with your goals, then you absolutely need to set up a system to help you stay within the parameters of your Spending and Savings Plan.

On Track Money Management System

Our On Track Money Management System is designed to help you do two things: a) stay on track with monthly and annual expenses; and b) save for your goals.

The system goes back to the old days of putting money into envelopes to make sure everything - from groceries to the gas bill - got paid. When payday rolled around, you'd put cash for groceries in one envelope, money for the bills in another, savings towards new clothes for school in yet another and so on.

To implement our system we suggest opening several bank accounts. Here's what we recommend:

1. One Main Chequing Account for fixed costs and regular monthly payments

2. A Monthly Spending Account for things you tend to spend money on every month

3. Several Savings accounts to save up for Lump Sum and Annual Expenses

Refer back to your Spending and Savings Plan and you will see that the Expenses Section has been divided into these three categories.

The idea is to use different bank accounts to create 'electronic' envelopes - so the car insurance money gets saved and not spent on pedicures, the account for university fees adds up instead of being drained by car repairs or other unexpected expenses. And the vacation budget, often a priority but usually the first to be sacrificed to overspending in other areas, gets stashed in an account labelled 'Travel,' safe from impulse shoe buying or unlimited lattes.

In effect, it doesn't just give you a budget to follow, it forces you to limit your spending in each category to the amount you have in the account. If you've determined that it costs you $800 a month for groceries and by the third week you're down to your last $60 in the Monthly Spending Account, no seeking solace in the credit card or pilfering other accounts. Get out the recipes and use up what's left in the cupboard.

ON TRACK MONEY MANAGEMENT SYSTEM

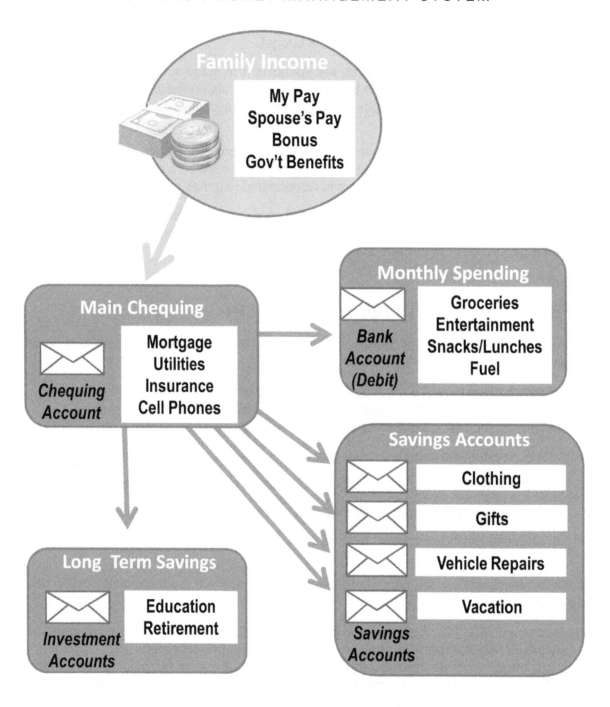

Consider the case of Jennifer, a client who confessed to constantly living in her overdraft. "I had no trouble putting together a budget based on what I had spent," she said. "I was spending more than I was bringing in and when annual expenses rolled around, it was a scramble to find the money to pay them.

"But when I started planning ahead for those annual expenses and putting away the money every month so I'd have money to pay them - wow, what a difference it made. No more panic when big annual bills came up and no more running up my credit cards to pay for them."

It took some discussion and hard decisions to set priorities. Jennifer opted for several accounts, because if there was money in a single account that had to cover several long-term items, there was a temptation to borrow from it with the expectation that money would magically appear to fill the account by a bill's due date. Some clients choose to manage with fewer savings accounts, but the key is to create clarity. Do I have money for clothes, or not? Have we spent the dining out money or is there still some left for Friday night?

The payoff can be huge. And not just in terms of money but of peace of mind.

"The first time my annual insurance bill came around and I actually had enough money in a savings account to pay it I realized my plan was working," said Jennifer. "And when I was able to book a vacation and pay for it with my Travel Savings instead of putting it off or putting it onto my credit card, I was thrilled. The spending guilt was gone. Now it's easy to make financial choices—I can walk by Manolo Blahniks on sale and keep walking because I know if I spend money on them, there goes the trip to Hawaii."

Implementing the On Track Money Management System

1. Main Chequing Account

The Goal: To separate your bill money from your spending money. Keep only enough in this account to cover your bills and regular monthly payments. This way you don't have to worry about spending the rent or mortgage money on groceries or clothes. The money stays in the Main Chequing Account until the bills need to be paid.

Monthly Fixed Costs are bills and regular payments that are approximately the same amount every month.

For example: rent, mortgage, phone and cable bills, car loan, newspaper subscription and monthly savings for RESP and RSP payments are all likely to be the same amount each month and thus considered 'fixed.'

The Plan

- Use your Main Chequing Account for monthly fixed costs.
- Deposit all income into your Main Chequing Account.
- Pay bills and expenses that are fixed and payable monthly from this account.
- Leave only enough money in this account to cover your bills and fixed costs for the month. You will find your total for your monthly fixed costs on your Spending and Savings Plan.
- Don't use this account for spending money; it's just for the bills.
- Leave a small buffer of say $50 to $100 per month to cover any variances in the bills.
- Take out overdraft protection on this account, but only use it in an absolute emergency.

Tips

- You may want to consider equal billing for utility bills like gas and electricity to help even out your expenses. You can arrange with the utility companies to pay a set amount every month to eliminate seasonal jumps in your bills. This allows you to more accurately predict your monthly costs.

- If you are self-employed we recommend setting up a separate chequing account to use for your business income and expenses. This will keep your business cash flow separate from your personal. To draw money from the business account we recommend transferring a regular pay or 'salary' to your personal account to mimic a paycheque. The amount must be fixed and drawn consistently i.e. once a month, 15th and 30th or every two weeks.

- If you are self-employed you also need to save for your 'holiday pay' to cover for your loss of income when away from work. This amount should be enough to cover your draw or 'salary' so you can continue to pay your bills and stick to your Spending and Savings Plan when you take time off.

2. Monthly Spending Account

The Goal: To keep your monthly spending within the limits that you set out in your Spending and Savings Plan. Open a second chequing account and give yourself a certain amount each pay period to spend on expenses that you know you will incur every month but want to keep to a specific amount to stay on track. You can spend what's in the account, but when it's gone, it's gone. Plan to cover all the expenses you need and want for each month and no more.

Monthly Spending includes expenses that you spend money on every month, but the amounts can be variable.

For example: You will likely need money every month for groceries, cleaning supplies, gas, bus, parking, entertainment, dining out and spending money but the amount you spend can vary from month to month.

Sue and Bob's planned monthly spending totalled $1,200. They transfer $600 per pay to their Monthly Spending Account. Their goal is to make this money last for two weeks. If they run out of money in the first week, it's rice and beans till payday.

And yes, Sue does feel like it is a bit limiting to have only so much to spend, but says "it's worth it" as it keeps them from overspending and frees up money for the things they really want, like a trip to Italy.

It works for them and Sue says "Every time I pass over the ice cream aisle I imagine myself sipping a latte on a sidewalk café in Venice!"

The Plan

- Use a second chequing account for Monthly Spending.
- The amount you have budgeted for monthly spending expenses can be found on your Spending and Savings Plan.
- Transfer this amount of money from your Main Chequing Account each payday.
- Use debit to access this account for your spending.
- This is your spending money for the month, make it last.
- Decline overdraft protection on this account so that when the account is empty, you have to stop spending.

Tip

- Transfer half the monthly amount needed on the 15th and 30th or every two weeks if you are paid bi-weekly. We find that two weeks is about as far out as people can plan with their monthly expenses. If you aren't able to stick to your plan and the money is spent in the first week, don't despair—there will be more transferred into your account within two weeks to keep you going for the rest of the month.

3. Savings Accounts—Lump Sum and Annual Expenses

The Goal: To set aside an amount every month for the expenses that occur irregularly or annually. By saving monthly for these expenses you should have the money available when you need it. This way you won't have to rely on credit cards or your line of credit when these expenses come up.

By having a separate account for each type of expense, you will know how much money you have available to spend in each category. It also keeps the money separate from your other spending so you don't accidentally spend your savings on something like dining out or lattes.

Lump Sum and Annual Expenses are those irregular expenses that come up once a year or sporadically throughout the year.

For example: Car repairs, property taxes, house insurance, clothes, gifts, travel, and vet bills are all things you may need or want to spend money on sometime throughout the year.

The Plan

- Review your Spending and Savings Plan for expenses that you have planned for in the Savings Accounts—Lump Sum and Annual Expenses section.

- Set up separate high-interest, no-fee savings accounts at your bank for each expense category that you want to save for.

- Nickname the accounts for the various expenses you need and want to save for.

- Divide the annual total you planned on spending in each category by the number of paydays you have in a year.

- Transfer this amount to the designated accounts each payday from your Main Chequing Account.

- Debit is usually unavailable on high-interest savings accounts, so when you make a purchase, you can access the funds in one of two ways:

    1. **Pay by Credit Card** and then pay off the credit card immediately from the designated savings account. Your credit card balance will be at zero (where we like to keep it) and the savings account balance is up to date with the remaining funds available for your next purchase.

    2. **Pay by Cheque** and then transfer the money from the designated savings account to your Main Chequing Account. The money should stay safe in the Main Chequing Account until the cheque is cashed, as this account is not for spending.

Tips

- When paying off the credit card for a lump sum or annual expense pay the exact amount you spent (e.g., $128.04) so that when the bills come it is easy to see which expenses have been paid for from the designated accounts, and which may have been missed.

- If your bank charges a fee to pay bills from your high-interest savings account it is better to transfer the amount first to your Main Chequing Account. Then pay the credit card bill from the Main Chequing Account as this account should have unlimited transactions. Transfers between accounts should be free.

Fixed Lump Sum and Annual Expenses

These can include all your annual expenses that have a fixed amount due each year. Since the amount for each bill is set, you can tally up all the costs that fit into this category and save for them in one account. Add up the totals and divide by your number of pay periods and start setting the money aside. If you get the timing right the money will be set aside in the account when each bill comes due.

Variable Lump Sum and Annual Expenses

Home Repairs or Major Purchases—renovations, painting, new furniture, stereo, lamps, sheets, curtains... How much do you need, or can you afford, to allocate to these types of expenses?

Car Repairs and Maintenance—include regular scheduled maintenance as well as things like new brakes, new tires, and the deductible on break-ins or car repairs from an accident.

Medical/Dental/Glasses/Contacts—if you have to pay for all or some of these expenses irregularly, start setting the money aside now. Don't forget massage, chiropractic, naturopath and physio.

Personal Care—if you have large expenses for hair, makeup or other personal care items, save monthly so the money is available when you need it.

Clothes—if you tend to do a few big shops per year it's nice to save up so you have the money before you go shopping. Then you know how much you can spend.

Gifts—Birthdays, Mother's Day, Father's Day, anniversary, Christmas, weddings, new babies, house warmings... Write out a schedule of holidays, birthdays and other miscellaneous events you buy gifts for. This could include expenses for family gatherings or birthday parties you host.

Children's Activities—List all the activities for your children and the associated costs throughout the year. Include amounts for summer camps, school trips, sports activities and equipment, music lessons, drama class etc.

Vet Bills—Plan for the costs of the annual checkup and regular shots plus the unexpected vet bill that may come up.

Travel—Include major vacations, trips back home, camping, weekend getaways etc. Set aside money monthly (and extra when you can) so there is money for these much-needed breaks. But remember, the rule is you can only spend what's in the account, so if there is only $549 in the travel account, it is a $549 vacation.

Self-Improvement or Hobbies—this can include anything from French classes, to yoga or photography to counseling or a course you might need to take for work.

Time off or Holiday Pay—If you are self-employed you also need to save for your 'holiday pay' to cover for your loss of income when away from work.

Annual or Lump Sum Expenses Worksheet

- Make a list of the annual or lump sum expenses you need or want to save for
- Tally up how much you think you will need or want to spend on these expenses in the next 12 months
- Divide the annual amount by the number of pay periods you have in a year (24 pay periods if you are paid on the 15th and 30th of the month or 26 pay periods if you are paid every two weeks)
- Set aside this amount each pay day to save for the things you need and want throughout the year
- See the next page for more detailed information about these expenses.

FIXED LUMP SUM AND ANNUAL EXPENSES	Estimated Amount Needed Per Year	Amount to Set Aside Each Payday
Property taxes	$_____	$_____
Vehicle insurance	$_____	$_____
Property Insurance	$_____	$_____
Clubs & Memberships (if paid annually)	$_____	$_____
Magazine Subscriptions	$_____	$_____
Costco Membership/Credit Card Fees	$_____	$_____
Professional / Accounting Fees	$_____	$_____

Total Fixed Lump Sum and Annual Expenses
(these can all be saved for in one account)

VARIABLE LUMP SUM AND ANNUAL EXPENSES (set up a separate account for each category needed)	Estimated Amount Needed Per Year	Amount to Set Aside Each Payday
HOME REPAIRS, FURNITURE, HOUSEHOLD ITEMS	$_____	$_____
VEHICLE REPAIRS AND MAINTENANCE	$_____	$_____
MEDICAL /DENTAL /GLASSES / CONTACTS	$_____	$_____
PERSONAL CARE	$_____	$_____
CLOTHING, SHOES, OUTERWEAR	$_____	$_____
GIFTS AND DONATIONS	$_____	$_____
CHILDREN'S ACTIVITIES	$_____	$_____
VET BILLS	$_____	$_____
TRAVEL, VACATIONS AND FAMILY FUN	$_____	$_____
SELF IMPROVEMENT OR HOBBIES	$_____	$_____
COMPUTER/ELECTRONICS	$_____	$_____
HOLIDAY PAY (If Self Employed)	$_____	$_____
OTHER: _____	$_____	$_____
OTHER: _____	$_____	$_____
OTHER: _____	$_____	$_____

Types of Accounts Recommended for the On Track Money Management System

Account	How Many do I need?	Purpose	Type of Bank Account	Features		How do I spend money out of this account?
				Debit Card Access?	Set up Overdraft?	
Main Chequing	One	Fixed Costs - Regular Monthly Payments and Bills (Rent/mortgage, hydro, phone, monthly insurance payments, etc.)	Chequing with unlimited transactions	No	Yes	Pre-authorized payments, bill payments, write cheques
Chequing #2	One	Monthly Spending (Groceries, gas, pet food, dining out, etc.)	Chequing with low fee Depending on how many times you shop, may want to have unlimited transactions	Yes	No	Debit card – point-of-sale purchases or withdraw cash
Savings	Several	Lump Sum and Annual Expenses (Clothing, gifts, property insurance, vacations, children's activities, etc.)	No fee high-interest savings accounts	No	No	Transfer money to credit card or main chequing account to cover purchases made (e.g., Buy clothing for $75.25 with credit card, transfer $75.25 to credit card from Clothing savings account)

By following the On Track Money Management System you not only achieve your goals, you do so without the stress of incurring debt.

Make Savings A Habit

"More people should learn to
tell their dollars where to go
instead of asking them
where they went."

~Roger Babson

You Just Have to Save

Being in control of your finances and saving for the things you want are synonymous. If you can't find money to save for your goals, then you aren't prioritizing your goals. And if you think you can get control *and keep control* without having any savings you are kidding yourself. One unexpected expense and you are going backwards again. After all your work so far - that would really hurt.

But saving money does more than stave off debt, which in and of itself is a good reason to save.

Seeing money in a bank account staves off fear. You don't have to worry that you are stuck, or that you can't live the life you want. It is a reminder that you are working towards your goals; that you have choices. It is a tangible link between you and your goals. And it's a progress report on your efforts.

Your income is important, but it is your savings that shows you are seriously in control of your life and your money.

Hints On Setting Reasonable Savings Goals

Plan to save for your goals. By now you know goals don't just happen. You make them happen. So set up the savings accounts and put your money where your heart is.

Plan to save for retirement. Most advisors suggest that you aim to save a minimum of 10% of your income for retirement alone. In the retirement planning section you'll find out what numbers are right for you. But for now, even $25 a month will improve your financial outlook significantly.

Plan to save for emergencies. A goal, which may or may not be on your goal's page, should be to set aside money for emergencies. By the way, an unexpected trip to Thailand is not an emergency. Ideally, your emergency fund should cover 3 to 6 months worth of expenses. If that seems like a daunting number, remember that you don't have to have it all by tomorrow - just start with whatever you can. Even if you have $300 in an emergency fund, it will keep you from sliding backwards and losing morale the first time your cat needs emergency surgery or you pop the side mirror off your car. Make an emergency fund a goal.

Creative Ways To Save

Pay yourself first! Set up automatic savings plans for your priority goals. Transfer the money, as soon as you get paid, before you spend the money on something you don't need!

Name your savings. No kidding! Once you name a gold fish you feel more attached to it - the same goes for your savings. Some banks will allow you to nickname your accounts so set up one for each of your goals: one for house, one for wedding, one for travel, etc. Naming the account not only helps you track how much you've saved for each goal, it makes your savings seem less like numbers in the bank, and more like friends you can check in on. And if you see $800 in an account named "Dream House", you will be hard pressed to steal money out of it to cover insignificant indulgences.

Money jars! Keep a jar at home for each of your goals. Name them, paint them, tape a picture to them to remind you of your goals (but don't spend money on them). If you opt not to eat out one night, put $20 in your "travel" jar instead. Or get in the habit of putting a Loonie in the "new couch" jar every day - water plants, brush teeth, feed the jar! Make your savings and your goals part of your life.

Karin got serious about her goal once she named her account.

For years I've heard Sheila teach people to set up bank accounts with "nicknames" for their goals. To be honest, I thought it was a little hokey!

But recently my husband and I started thinking seriously about buying a property on Salt Spring Island. We had some savings that we could allocate to it, so I thought I'd give Sheila's idea a try. I set up an investment savings account, named the account "Salt Spring Home" put $3,000 into the fund and started making monthly transfers.

I kid you not, within 3 months of opening the account, we found a property on Salt Spring, put in an offer, found the rest of the down payment money and bought a fantastic house, way before we ever imagined we would. I'm convinced that by giving the savings account a name and putting money into the account, we put out a very strong message that we were committed to our dream. So, what are you ready to make happen?

Let the bank help. You can shop around for a bank that offers low or no fee saving accounts. Better yet choose a bank that gives you interest! Online accounts offer 1-2% interest now. It feels really good to see the bank add money to your account each month.

Save the income from your first hour of work of every week. How hard can that be? Say you make $25 / hr. When you get to work on Monday morning, get in the habit of going online and transferring $25 from your chequing to your savings account. You'll start your work week by reminding yourself what you are working for and you'll be $100 richer for the experience each and every month.

If Mondays aren't good, do it before you leave work on Friday as a reward for a week's work, or mid day on Wednesdays, to help get you over the hump.

There's really no excuse not to save. You can do it. It can be fun. It's part of taking control.

How much can you commit to saving today?   _____

Put Your Savings Goals In Your Spending and Savings Plan

Pull out your Goals pages and your Spending and Savings Plan now.

Take a hard look at how much you are currently saving for your goals and challenge yourself to find just a little bit more money for your savings.

Can you set $25 a month aside for art classes? $100 for the new condo? $125 for travel?

Don't get too excited and stash away so much cash that you can't pay for your necessary monthly expenses. You need to keep in mind that there is no need to go into debt over day-to-day purchases.

Just look at your expenses and ask yourself what is really necessary? What can I turn into savings? And make the necessary revisions to your Spending and Savings Plan now.

Do your best to be your best.

You and Your Credit

Get out of debt

and

stay out

of debt.

Don't argue.

A Good Credit History is Important

Using credit wisely is critical to building a solid credit history. Your credit history is what banks and other creditors use to assess how risky it would be to lend you money. The way you have handled your debts in the past will affect a lender's decision to lend you money and affect the amount of interest they will charge you. If you need a loan or a mortgage, or you need to renegotiate a loan, you want to be able to choose your lender and negotiate your lending rate. You want control.

Know where you stand. In Canada, your credit history is tracked by two major credit tracking companies: *Equifax* and *TransUnion*. They keep records of: where you work, how much debt you have, whether you've paid your debt on time, and also how much credit you have available. Every time you apply for a loan or credit, the financial institution will request a credit history report from one of these companies.

You can contact these companies too. Request a copy of the information that they have on file. Make sure the information they have is accurate, and that you aren't being haunted by a forgotten unpaid bill.

www. transunion.ca   **www.equifax.ca**

Your credit history can be connected to other people (past and present). If you co-signed a loan that wasn't paid, it will affect your credit history. If your name is still on a credit card that your ex is using that will also affect your credit. If your children have cell phones under your name and they are ditching their bills, you might pay the price when it comes time to refinance your mortgage.

If you have never had credit of any kind, if you are just starting out, or if you have always had credit in your partner's name, you won't have a credit history. Since there is no way for a potential lender to assess the risk associated with lending to you, you might find it very challenging to get a loan if, and when, you need one. It is a good idea to have some well-managed credit in your name.

You don't need 5 credit cards to have a good credit history. You just need to show that you can manage debt responsibly and pay on time.

If you have hiccups in your history, don't panic. Lenders often give you a chance to explain if there were extraordinary circumstances. (Going to Thailand for 6 months and ditching your bills is extraordinarily bad practice but it isn't really what a lender would consider extraordinary circumstances.) You can explain an unpaid bill that was lost in the mail or a temporary period of missed payments immediately following an accident. And if you can demonstrate a marked improvement in your financial dealings post-hiccup, you will be in a much stronger position overall.

Responsible Debt Management

Responsible debt management gives you more choices and more financial freedom.

Borrowing has become a way of life. Our buy-now-pay-later culture seems to accept debt, and the costs associated with it, as part of the cost of living. It is important to remember that although nearly half of Canadian families spend more than they earn, the flip side to that statistic is that more than half don't. You need to decide for yourself how comfortable you are with debt and credit and not be swayed by what the Jones' are up to. (You never know how well they sleep at night, do you?)

Stores and businesses have made having credit a necessary convenience. Even if you don't think of it as borrowing, you are using your credit when you pay in installments on your insurance, or use your credit card to automatically pay your phone bill or reserve a hotel room. There's nothing wrong with taking advantage of these conveniences, so long as you do it responsibly.

Given the interest rates they can charge, creditors today are all too happy to lend money. If you get credit card offers in the mail every week, it's not because they think you are special. And they aren't being neighbourly. Creditors make lots and lots of money from people who are sloppy at paying their bills, or who buy into the idea that paying a little interest is a cost of living.

If you can't pay off your credit card each month, don't use credit. You are just emptying your pockets to line the creditor's pocket. Would you like to pay for their retirement home too? Don't you have your own life to pay for?

Your Line of Credit isn't your money. Bank statements and internet banking sites often make your Line of Credit look like any other account. Instead of having neon flashing lights saying, "This is money you owe us!", they often start off with, "Your amount of credit available." It is a nuance that costs some people a lot of money. Don't treat your Line of Credit (or your overdraft) like any other chequing or savings account. It's not your money.

These accounts are bridging or emergency resources only, and because they usually have a competitive interest rate, they can be very useful for those purposes. If your kitchen sink springs a leak while you are at work and you come home to find the downstairs neighbour has called a very expensive plumber who only deals in cash, you might need to draw some cash out of your Line of Credit. Okay, but when you use it, remember that it is a loan and you want to put a plan in place to pay it back.

When you use credit wisely (read: pay your bills on time every month) you amplify your life choices. You build a solid credit history and you demonstrate your financial control. All you have to do is make sure you have cash in the bank to cover your monthly loan payments and anything *and everything* you put on credit. You can do that - it is in your plan.

Good Debt vs. Bad Debt

The less debt you have the better. That being said, you will hear people talking about good debt vs. bad debt. Put simply,

> **Good debt** is used to buy assets - your house, your RSP, something with real value that you could sell if you needed to clear the debt.

> **Bad debt** is incurred when you weren't really looking. Your living expenses exceeded your income and you don't have an asset or any one thing that you could sell to clear the debt.

When interest rates are low, people talk about "cheap money". You might be tempted to take on debt now because you think it won't cost you as much as when interest rates are higher. Maybe, but if you aren't financially or emotionally prepared for your debt, you need to remember that overdue payments, damage to your credit, sleepless nights, stress and lack of freedom all add to the cost of borrowing.

It may be necessary to incur debt to attain your goals (e.g. a mortgage for a house). That's OK. The key is that you stay in control of your debt and that you stick to your plan to pay it off.

Trust Your Plan

You might be surprised by how much money lenders are willing to offer you. If you go for a mortgage pre-approval, you are likely to be approved for more than you think you can afford because lenders apply generic formulas to your income, debt load and credit history. They don't know the details of your monthly expenses.

Don't rely on a lender to tell you what you can, or can't afford.

If you don't think you can handle the loan payments associated with a purchase, trust your gut and your plan. They don't know you. They don't know what other goals you are working to achieve.

Borrow only what you need, and what you can foreseeably pay back. If lenders offer you more, great. You can still walk out with the amount of money *you chose* and the knowledge that even in the face of temptation, you chose to protect your future, and your sanity, by not taking on more than you can handle.

Get Out of Debt

No matter what the reason for the debt, so-called "good" or "bad" debt limits your options. It is as simple as that.

When you owe money, you have to make principal payments and interest payments monthly. That commits a significant portion of your income and limits your choices. Nothing causes more stress than being stuck in a job you hate because you need the pay cheque to service your debt load.

Buy yourself the freedom you deserve. Don't think of debt payment as punishment or you'll hate paying it. Taking control is about opening up possibilities. Paying off debt is a really good thing.

> "The price of anything is the amount of life you exchange for it."
> ~Henry Thoreau

Creative Ways to Get Out and Stay Out of Debt

Make paying down debt a #1 priority. It's not going to happen on its own. Consciously make an effort to pay down debt each month. You can take control!

Make debt reduction systematic. Use a jar. Use an automatic payment system at the bank. Commit to walking to the bank once a week with a cheque to yourself. Whatever makes you feel good and gets the job done. You'll know your system is working when you see your debt and your stress steadily decrease.

Keep a running tally of your debt. Track the balance on your debt each month. Make sure it is going down, not just staying the same. When you see it go down, you'll think twice about racking it back up.

Shop around for a lower interest rate. Reduce your interest rate by all means. Don't reduce your commitment to be debt free.

Tackle one debt at a time. Throwing $100 a month at 5 different debts can cost you money and momentum. You won't see any serious progress, meanwhile you are paying interest on everything. Put the majority of your resources into one debt and make the minimum payments on everything else. You will feel great when you can cross the first debt off your list!

Pay down the debt with the highest interest rate first. The sooner you can get rid of high interest credits cards and debt, the more progress you'll make.

Pay off your credit cards in full each month. If you can't:

> **Stop using your credit cards.** It may be the only way. Start using cash. If you have to use your credit card, go home, go online and transfer the money from your bank to your credit card immediately! This way you'll think before you spend, "Do I really have money for this?"

Consolidate all debt to one loan or line of credit at the lowest possible rate. This will reduce your interest charges significantly, but if you continue to use your credit cards irresponsibly you'll dig yourself deeper in the hole. Don't consolidate your loans until you have proven to yourself that your financial thinking *and your financial habits* have changed for good!

Did you know ...

A $10,000 debt on a credit card charging **19.5%** interest

costs you **$1,950 in interest each year.**

If you move the same **$10,000** debt to a line of credit at **9%**

you will save yourself over $1,000 and get out of debt that much faster!

Set a date to be debt-free. This is fun. Really. When you know the date, you can see the end.

Reducing her debt and reducing her stress was Kate's #1 goal.

	Debt	Original Mo. Payment	Recommended Mo. Payment
Line of Credit Balance	$6,000 @9%	$180	$180 + $200 = $380
Car loan (48 months)	$14,000 @7%	$335	$335
Total Debt	$20,000	$515	$715

Kate had $20,000 in combined debt on her Line of Credit and car loan but she wanted to be debt-free in 2.5 years so she could buy a home.

She wanted to pay down the loan with the highest interest first, so she decided to keep making the minimum payments on her car loan and focus any available resources on paying off her Line of Credit.

After talking to her bank (and using her bank's on-line calculator) she figured out that if she increased her monthly payments by only $200 she could have her Line of Credit paid out in less than 18 months. That is 21 months faster than if she had continued to pay just $180/mo.

Once she paid off her Line of Credit, she added that money ($380) to the monthly payments on her car loan ($335). The extra funds made it possible to shed that debt a whole year ahead of schedule.

By simply increasing her payments by $200 a month, or $50 per week (the cost of a few lunches out) Kate was able to accelerate her debt-free date from 4 years to 2.5 years. Shemade fantastic progress toward her goals and saved over $950 in interest as well!

Instructions for Setting a Debt-Free Date

Take out your Net Worth and use the next page to add up your debts. Start by writing down the payments you are currently making and figure out how many months it will take to be debt-free.

It might be sooner than you think. Or, if it is going to take longer than you would like to pay off your debt, see what adding an extra $50 a week to one debt would do to your time line. It may not sound like much but look how much it did for Kate!

Hint: Talk to your lender about how long it will take you to pay out your loan based on the payments you make now, and ask what payment options you have. Or use a calculator on your bank's web site.

Lender	Debt	Interest	Your Repayment Plan $x / month for x many months
E.g. Car Loan	$10,000	9%	$200 a month for 60 months
E.g. Line of Credit	$10,000	9%	$310 a month for 36 months
_____	_____	_____	_____
_____	_____	_____	_____
_____	_____	_____	_____
_____	_____	_____	_____

Total Debt = _____   Total Months to Debt-free =_____

Do you like the answer? Is it the best answer for you? If not, review the Creative Ways to Get Out and Stay Out of Debt section. Try to imagine what you could do differently and then make adjustments.

I want to be debt-free by _____

FYI: Your debt-free date calculation only works if you stop adding to your debt. The minute you add to your debt, you push back your date to be debt-free.

Put Your Debt Repayment Goals In Your Spending and Savings Plan

To determine how much can you comfortably commit to your debt each month you'll need to once again pull out your Goals pages and your Spending and Savings Plan. See how useful these things are?

Take a hard look at how much you have allocated for paying down your debts and challenge yourself to find that little bit more. You might think there's nothing left, but review your goals and remember that debt limits your choices. If you are tired of cutting, are you inspired to earn a little more? Make the changes you need to live the life you want. Write them down on your plan and start putting them into action!

Stay flexible, think creatively, grow.

Invest in Yourself

The Basics of Investing

Investing is simply a tool to help you live the life you want.

In this section, you will learn the basics of investing and discover that it really is simpler than you think.

If you are new to investing, and even if you're not, it wouldn't be unusual for you to feel overwhelmed by the sheer number of investment choices available to you, and then there's the lingo! But don't let the numbers, the choices, or the weird words intimidate you.

In our experience, approximately 90% of you will work with investment advisors when it comes time to invest. The information provided here isn't intended to make you an overnight investment expert. It will help you feel more confident in selecting and working with your financial planners and investment advisors. And it will give you the big picture so that you can **delegate, not abdicate**, the responsibility for the management of your investments.

Here's how it usually works:

- Some investment decisions you'll make on your own

- Some investment decisions you'll make in consultation with your advisor

- And some decisions you will delegate to your advisor, knowing that you have built a plan that fits your needs, reviewed your plan with your advisor, and chosen an advisor who will make decisions on your behalf that work within the parameters of your plan.

So if you are wondering if investments are for you - they are. The real question is: which investments, and investment advisor, are best for you. This chapter will help you start to find your answers.

A Quick Word About Risk

Many people stay away from investing in anything beyond a savings or GIC account because it seems risky. Specifically, they fear the risk of losing their *capital*, or initial investment. But there are other risks you need to consider:

- Risk that your investment may not keep up with inflation

- Risk of putting all your eggs in one basket

- Risk of outliving your savings

Your Investment Plan should reflect the level of risk you can live with. That means striking a balance. You don't want to be pacing the floors because your money is in stocks that you fear will crash. Neither do you want to be pacing the floors because you don't have enough money for a decent mattress in your golden years!

A well thought out Investment Plan will support you to make sound decisions, rather than decisions based on emotions, fear or market fluctuations. If you are a new investor, you might find that you have very little tolerance for investment risk. That's okay. As you gain education and experience investing, you will likely become more comfortable taking the appropriate amount of risk to achieve your goals.

Investments and investment plans are not one-size-fits-all. Listen and learn from others, but don't think you can just pick the same investments your sister picks, or your neighbour, or your colleague at work; you may all have very different risk profiles and different visions for your life.

What Your Money Can Do For You

Money can't buy happiness, but when you invest your money it can do these three things:

It can provide **safety**.

Safety investments protect your initial investment. In some cases it will even be guaranteed. Safety is usually a key consideration for short term goals like saving for a down payment for a home, or a vacation.

It can provide **income**.

Income investments are set up to pay you an income on a regular basis. This is primarily an option for an investor who has a larger sum of money to invest, and wants to use some or all of the income earned on the investment for their monthly cash flow. This is often a key consideration at retirement.

It can **grow**.

Growth investments increase in value over time. The key here is "over time". Growth investments will go through ups and downs. Ideally, your payoff for riding out the ups and downs is a better return on your investment. Growth is usually a key consideration for long term goals such as saving for retirement.

Most people benefit from having a mix of safety, income and growth investments.

Investing with Class

All investments are categorized and the categories are referred to as *Asset Classes.* Most investments fall into 3 main Asset Classes.

Cash This class includes more than just the cash in your pocket or the cash in your chequing account. It refers to investments that tend to be short term and *liquid* in nature, meaning you can easily access the money without risking a loss in the value of the investment.

Examples include:

> Savings accounts
> GICs (Guaranteed Investment Certificates)
> TDs (Term Deposits)
> Money Market Accounts

Cash investments have the lowest risk and lowest potential return.

Bonds A bond is actually an IOU. You agree to loan money to the government, or to a company, and they agree to pay you a specified amount of interest at regular intervals (usually twice a year), *and* repay the loan on a specified date. When that date comes up, the bond is said to have *matured*. At maturity, you are paid the bond's *face value*, which is the amount printed on the bond.

Though bonds are generally quite safe, there are some risks. The company you loan money to *could* go bankrupt and be unable to pay you back. If interest rates rise, your fixed interest rate *could* earn less than the going rate. And although you can get your money out of a bond by selling it, if your sale is poorly timed, the bond *could* be valued for less than your principal investment.

Bond investments generally have medium risk and medium potential return.

Stocks (also known as *Equities*) If you own *stocks*, you actually own a piece of a company. Each piece is called a *share* and you are a *shareholder*.

Stocks could potentially benefit you in two ways:

> 1) Your Stock Value Increases: If the value of your stock goes up over time, your stocks could become worth more than you paid for them. And if at that point you sell your stocks, the difference between your purchase price and your selling price is a type of earnings called *Capital Gains*. Of program, if you don't sell, you can still benefit from seeing a stock value rise. As the value of your asset increases you improve your Net Worth!

> 2) You Receive Dividends: When an established company makes a profit, it may choose to pay the profit out to its shareholders, rather than invest it back into the company. These payments are called *dividends*. Dividends are often paid quarterly.

Of program the flip side is that:

> 1) Your Stock Value Decreases: If you have to sell your stocks at a time when they are worth less than what you initially paid, you incur *Capital Losses*, which is a fancy way of saying you've lost some or all of your initial investment. And just as your Net Worth improves when the asset gains value, your Net Worth decreases if the asset loses value.

> 2) No More Dividends: If the company stops making a profit, or if it goes through a change and decides to reinvest the profit in the company, it can stop paying dividends. At that point you could be out of an income stream.

Stock investments generally have higher risk and higher potential return.

Though we will cover Registered Savings Plans (RSPs) in more detail later, for now it is important to note that you can purchase investments in each of these Asset Classes in both Registered and Non-Registered accounts.

The Risk-Return Trade-Off

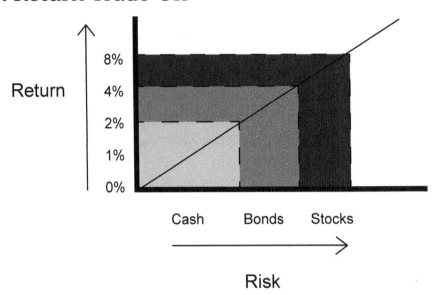

This chart demonstrates that *over time* the higher the investment risk, the higher the potential return.

Over the past 10 years, cash investments have earned an average 2% return on investment. Bonds averaged 4%. And stocks averaged 8%.* But it is important to keep in mind these are *averages* and higher risk investments swing more than lower risk investments. So although stock investments have averaged 10% over 10 years, some years you might see returns in the 20% range and some years in the -20% range.

Volatility: **the amount an investment fluctuates in value in a short period of time.**

You and your investments are bound to experience some ups and downs. Stocks are said to be more *volatile* than cash or bonds, because they are more likely to experience frequent swings in value, during short periods of time.

So why would people take the risk? Because they have the potential to earn more in the long run. If you are nervous about the stock market, remember this: companies are in business to make money and typically if they make money, you make money.

Throughout recorded history, the stock market has consistently outperformed government bonds and guaranteed investments. But if you plan to invest in more volatile investments, you have to have a long time horizon (7 years or more), some market literacy and confidence.

An Easy Way In

Mutual Funds are an easy way to invest in any *or all* of the asset classes. Instead of buying a single bond or stock, you pool your money with a lot of other investors to buy *units*, or shares of a mutual fund.

Mutual funds are managed by mutual fund companies. And mutual fund companies watch the markets

* Figures as of December 31, 2013. Numbers have been rounded. Sources: 91 Day TBill Index, Globe Fixed Income Peer Index, S&P/TSX Total Return Index.

very carefully. They use the pool of investor money to buy (and sell) Cash, Bonds and Stocks on a massive scale, much larger than any average investor. Then they group products together to achieve strategic investment objectives.

Some mutual funds will only include assets from a particular asset classification. If a mutual fund is made up of Cash assets, it would be considered a lower risk fund. A mutual fund that is comprised of a variety of stocks would fall into a higher risk category.

Mutual funds that hold a mix of Cash, Bonds, and Stocks are generally called *Balanced Funds*.

The value of a mutual fund is affected by the value of all the individual investments in the fund. So if your mutual fund is made up of 12 stocks, and 10 go up, while two go down, in theory, you will enjoy a value increase and you won't feel the burn of those two individual dips. Generally, balanced funds take this a step further because they combine lower risk investments with higher risk investments, thus reducing the overall risk of the investment.

Mutual funds have many advantages for the average investor.

Affordability Most mutual fund companies have low minimum investment amounts; you can start investing with as little as $25.

Monthly Contributions Mutual funds are designed for you to be able to make monthly contributions. The market changes every day. Some people wait to invest because they think they have to "time" their purchase strategically. But if you automatically invest a constant amount each month, say $50, the price fluctuations mean that some months you will buy more units than others with the same amount of cash. Over time, you average out the ups and the downs, so market timing isn't an issue. (More on this later!)

Diversification Diversification simply means that you don't have all your eggs in one basket. The idea behind the mutual fund is that by grouping investments together in a single fund, the mutual fund company protects its investors from the value swings of any single investment. This spreads out your risk. And if you invest in more than one type of mutual fund, you spread the risk even further.

Expertise Mutual funds are managed by professional money managers who have the experience, do the research and watch the trends.

Disclosure Stringent regulations outline how mutual funds must be set up and managed, and how investors are informed. Before you invest you will be given a document called a *prospectus,* which itemizes fees and lists the investments in the mutual fund. Once you invest, you will be sent regular statements on the performance of your investment.

Flexibility You can easily buy and sell your units in a mutual fund. You aren't locked in.

International investments It can be hard for the average investor to buy stocks and bonds outside of Canada (with the exception of the US). Mutual funds make it easy, and again, a knowledgeable professional is monitoring the international markets for you.

Some people mistakenly assume that mutual funds are higher risk investments, but that isn't necessarily the case. The risk associated with any mutual fund is determined by the investments in the fund, therefore they can be low, medium or high risk. And whether you are looking for safety, income or growth from your investment, you can likely find a mutual fund to fit your needs.

A Note On Real Estate

Real Estate is actually an asset class all its own. There are a few ways you can invest in real estate:

Primary Residence you can own your own home

Rental Property you can buy a property and rent it out

Recreational Property you can buy a cottage, hobby farm or time-share

Real Estate Investment Trust (REIT) you can buy shares in a real estate Company that holds income-producing properties. This investment option is highly regulated and REITs must distribute their profit as dividends.

Real estate is a hot topic these days. It is doing well now, and has done so historically, but it still has risks. Property values tend to cycle through ups and downs and they are very dependent on the overall economy of the region.

Owning your home has significant long term advantages but you still need to look carefully at how an investment in real estate impacts your overall plan. It is important that you give real estate careful consideration and not assume it is a "must have" investment.

Most people buy homes to live in; the investment advantages are a bonus. Whether you are looking at real estate for personal use, or strictly as an investment, be sure to think long term and ask yourself:

- Is this investment consistent with my goals?

- Can I maintain or increase the value of the investment? (Maintenance, decor, landscaping)

- Can I afford the monthly payments, and maintenance, and live the life I want?

- Do I have an emergency fund for unexpected maintenance?

- Am I prepared to be someone's landlord (If you are thinking of renting the property out)?

Consider the sheer size of the investment (it is a large amount of money to be allocated to a single investment). And consider the fact that you can't really access the money in the investment until you sell. By comparison, if you had the same amount of money invested in mutual funds, and you needed to withdraw 10% of it for any reason, you could sell 10% of your mutual funds. You can't sell your bathroom. Of program, you can't bathe the baby in a mutual fund either. It is worth factoring in that home ownership translates to security for a lot of people and that can be worth more than any investment advantage.

A Special Note For First Time Home Buyers

If you are a first time buyer, and you have RSPs, you may be eligible to use the Home Buyers' Plan to withdraw up to $25,000 from your RSP to buy your first home. If you take advantage of this opportunity, you have to repay the total amount withdrawn from your RSP within 15 years and your minimum annual repayment is 1/15 of the total. Say you withdrew the full $25,000, your minimum repayment would be $1,667 per year, or $139 per month. If you are unable to repay it, the annual repayment amount will be added to your taxable income for the year.

What is Your Money Doing For You?

If you currently have investments, it is important to take stock of what they are doing for you. Once again, you need to know where you stand today so that you can see what, if any, changes you should make for tomorrow. So where are your investment dollars right now? What are they doing?

Instructions to Complete the Current Investment Worksheets

Get your bank statements, investment statements and your defined contribution pension statement.

Look at your statements to find the current Market Value of your investments and fill that in on your worksheet. Note: The way information about your investments is presented in your statements will vary from one financial institution to another. If you need help reading the statement, don't be embarrassed. Even Certified Financial Planners find some statements frustrating to read. Call your investment advisor and ask them to tell you how to find the information you need.

If you were very detailed filling out your Net Worth you may just need to transfer the information over, but if you generalized you can take the time now to be specific.

Use one sheet for investments that you have in Registered Plans, such as RSPs and pensions. Use the other sheet for investments that you keep outside of your registered plans, such as savings accounts.

List the amount of money you currently have saved in each investment. Write the name and the amount of each of your investments in the appropriate column of Cash, Bonds or Stocks. Tally the columns to see how much you have invested in each asset class. Then tally your total amount invested overall.

If you have any Balanced funds, write on the worksheet that 50% of the investment is in bonds and 50% is in stocks. That may not be exact but it will be ok for the purposes of this exercise.

Finally, to get a percentage for each column, divide the total for each column by the total amount you have invested. If you have $2,000 invested in Cash, and $10,000 invested overall, you divide:

$2,000 divided by $10,000 = 0.20   **which means that 20% of your investments are in Cash**

Hints for Completing the Current Investment Worksheets

Savings accounts are investments. They might not earn very much return but when you chose to put money into a savings account, and keep it separate from the money you use for daily life, you have made an investment decision.

Pensions are investments. If you have a defined contribution pension through your work, don't forget about it when you look at the ways that you are investing. The way it is invested and the amount you have accumulated will affect other investment decisions that you make.

Ask if you don't know. If you don't know how your money is invested, this is the time to find out. Call your bank or your investment advisor and ask them to help you fill in this worksheet. Explain that you are reviewing your investments and you want to know how your money is invested. If they take the opportunity to try to sell you something, say that once you have a better understanding of what you have already bought, you will get back to them. You are in the driver's seat. It is your money.

HOW ARE YOU CURRENTLY INVESTED in Registered investments?

CASH (eg. Bank Accounts, Canada Savings Bonds, GICs, Term Deposits, Money Market Mutual Funds)		BONDS / INCOME (eg. Government or Corporate Bonds, Bond or Income Mutual Funds)		STOCKS / EQUITY / SHARES (eg. Individual Stocks, Equity Mutual Funds or Employee Share Purchase Plan)	
Investment	$ Amount	Investment	$ Amount	Investment	$ Amount
E.g. CIBC Money Market Mutual Fund	$1,000			E.g. Ethical International Equity Fund	$10,000
Total Cash Type Investments:	$0.00	**Total Bond Type Investments:**	$0.00	**Total Stock Type Investments:**	$0.00
	%		%		%

Total Investments $0.00

HOW ARE YOU CURRENTLY INVESTED in NON-Registered investments?

CASH (eg. Bank Accounts, Canada Savings Bonds, GICs, Term Deposits, Money Market Mutual Funds)		BONDS / INCOME (eg. Government or Corporate Bonds, Bond or Income Mutual Funds)		STOCKS / EQUITY / SHARES (eg. Individual Stocks, Equity Mutual Funds or Employee Share Purchase Plan)	
Investment	$ Amount	Investment	$ Amount	Investment	$ Amount
E.g. ING Investment savings	$1,500				
Total Cash Type Investments:	$0.00	Total Bond Type Investments:	$0.00	Total Stock Type Investments:	$0.00
	%		%		%

Total Investments $0.00

Dividing Up Your Investment Dollars

Dividing up your investment dollars between Cash, Bond or Stock investments is called *asset allocation*. If you had to use both pages of the Current Investment worksheets, or multiple columns on a single page, you have already begun allocating your assets. Now, you get to find out if you have allocated them to your best advantage!

Asset allocation is a key part of your investment plan because it helps you balance risk and return and maximize the potential for your investments to support your goals and your life. People who go ahead without an asset allocation plan are really speculating, not investing, and if you want to talk about risk, speculating is risky business.

It is unlikely that a single investment will meet all of your investment needs. It is possible that you will find a single investment for each of your goals, and it is also possible that for a single goal, you will opt to invest in a combination of investments. The combination of investments you choose is your *investment portfolio.*

Remember, you want to achieve your goals but you also want to achieve well being, so you can't underestimate the importance of including your risk tolerance in your plans.

Frank plans to retire in 30 years. He has $30,000 already saved, but he has just been moving his money from one GIC to another because he didn't understand his investment options and was afraid of losing his money in higher risk investments.

Now Frank's ready to invest to his best advantage. He's thought it through and although retirement is a long term goal, he's only starting to build his understanding and confidence with the market. He says he has a medium risk tolerance.

A possible asset allocation for his scenario could be: 10% cash, 30% bonds and 60% equities.

Why? Frank doesn't need much in the way of cash investments for this goal because retirement is a long way away, and he **now** knows that he is comfortable with medium risk investments. Bonds are a good medium risk investment but they don't give him the growth he could get in Equities. Since he has a long time horizon, and some lower risk investments that should stay steady through market dips, investing 60% in equities will maximize his investment's growth potential, while respecting his risk tolerance and his goal.

This strategy could be applied equally to the money he has already saved, and to the money he plans to invest each month.

Many experts say that it is not the individual funds you choose that determine the overall success of your Investment Plan, but rather the degree to which you have maximized the benefits of all three asset classes to achieve your goals.

Again, It Goes Back To Your Goals

Your investment decisions must suit the needs of your overall financial plan. And so, as with your financial plan, we encourage you to design your Investment Plan goal by goal. There are a lot of investment options out there, but it is easier to make sense of which ones are right for you when you attach your investment decisions to specific goals.

There is no "right" investment or Investment Plan for everyone. Listen and learn from others, but don't think you can just pick the same investments your sister picks; she might have a very different risk profile, or vision for her life, than you do.

The central questions for investing are:

- What is the money for? (see your goals sheets)

- When do I need the money? (see your goals sheets)

- What investment, or portfolio of investments, would best suit this goal?

- Is my tolerance for risk compatible with this investment / portfolio?

Lacey and her sisters are saving up to host their parents' 40th wedding anniversary. The sisters are spread out all over Canada so it will be a big surprise to have the whole family together.

They need enough money to fly all four sisters and their families to Regina, host a dinner reception for 40 people, and pay for hotel rooms and little extras. And they want to build up a kitty so that they can promise their parents that they'll all be together again for their 50th.

Their goal is to have $12,000 within 12 months for the 40th anniversary party, and save another $8,000 over 10 years.

They are savvy people and they came up with a great investment strategy.

All four sisters contribute $250 a month to savings accounts. In 12 months, they will have saved enough to pay for the 40th anniversary.

Also they pooled their money and bought $4,000 of stock mutual funds, which they hope will average an 8% return. At that rate, they could more than double their investment in 10 years.

By putting 60% of their investment money into safer investments (e.g. savings accounts), they guarantee they will have money for the short term part of their goal. And by putting 40% of their money into stock mutual funds, they are letting the market pay for half of the next celebration! Although they know there are no guarantees with stock mutual funds, they are comfortable taking the risk for this long term goal.

See how Lacey used the "Which Investments Are Right For Me?" worksheet on the next page to figure out how they would save the $12,000 for the 40th anniversary party.

WHICH INVESTMENTS ARE RIGHT FOR ME?
*Using Lacy's example from the previous page.

Goal #1

Step 1: What are my investment objectives?

Ask yourself 3 Questions:
1. Why am I Saving?
(Ex. House, Vacation, Retirement)   40th Anniversary Party

2. When do I need the money?

Within 1 Yr	X
2 - 5 years	
5 - 10 years	
10 years or more	

3. What am I Looking For?
- Rank in order of priority 1, 2, o

Safety	1
Income	n/a
Growth	n/a

Step 2: What is My Risk Tolerance?
How comfortable am I with Volatility?
Check One:

Not Very (Low Risk)	X
Quite Comfortable (Medium)	
Very Comfortable (High)	

Step 3: What is my Asset Allocation?
Given my investment objective and risk tolerance, how much do I want to invest in:

Cash	100%
Bonds	0%
Stocks	0%
	100%

Step 4: How much money can I put towards this goal?

Total saved to date	Nothing Yet
Monthly contribution	$250 x 4 sisters = $1000/month

Step 5: What is my plan of action for investing this money?
My sisters and I will each open a high-interest savings account at our local banks and we will each set up an automatic monthly payment of $250 for the next 12 months

Instructions For Creating Goal-Centred Investment Plans

For each of your goals you are going decide, "Which Investments Are Right For Me?" You will answer all the central investing questions and create a plan of action for each goal. Worksheets are provided for your top three goals. And again, use pencil.

Pull out your Goals, Spending and Savings Plan and Your Current Investment worksheets.

For a quick reference, use this chart to help you match your goals to your investment options.

Asset Class and Asset Allocation Summary

Asset Class	Your Objective	Types of Investments	Risk	Advantage
Cash	Safety	• Savings and Chequing accounts • Canada Savings Bonds • Money Market Mutual Funds • GICs (Guaranteed Investment Certificates • Term Deposits	Long run inflation	Liquidity Safety
Bonds	Income	• Bonds • Bond or Fixed Income Mutual Funds	Mid term volatility Long run inflation	Fixed income Diversification
Stocks	Growth	• Stocks / Equities • Stock / Equity Mutual Funds	Short term volatility	Long term growth Hedge against inflation

And yes, you might make some changes to your Spending and Savings Plan. Now that you have a better understanding of the ways that you can make your money work for you, do you want to find a bit more for investing? Or do you need to adjust the targets you set for savings?

This is numbers stuff, but don't forget to keep your creative hat on. If you encounter a hurdle, either to completing the plans or to achieving your goal, take a good look at the obstacle and imagine how you can get over it.

WHICH INVESTMENTS ARE RIGHT FOR ME?

Step 1: What are my investment objectives?   Goal #1

      Ask yourself 3 Questions:
1. **Why am I Saving?**
      (Ex. House, Vacation, Retirement)   _____

2. **When do I need the money?**

Within 1 Yr	_____
2 - 5 years	_____
5 - 10 years	_____
10 years or more	_____

3. **What am I Looking For?**
      - Rank in order of priority 1, 2, o

Safety	_____
Income	_____
Growth	_____

Step 2: What is My Risk Tolerance?
      How comfortable am I with Volatility?
      Check One:

Not Very (Low Risk)	_____
Quite Comfortable (Medium)	_____
Very Comfortable (High)	_____

Step 3: What is my Asset Allocation?
      Given my investment objective and risk tolerance, how much do I want to invest in:

Cash	_____	%
Bonds	_____	%
Stocks	_____	%
	100%	

Step 4: How much money can I put towards this goal?
      Total saved to date _____
      Monthly contribution _____

Step 5: What is my plan of action for investing this money?

_____

_____

_____

WHICH INVESTMENTS ARE RIGHT FOR ME?

Goal #2

Step 1: What are my investment objectives?

Ask yourself 3 Questions:
1. **Why am I Saving?**
    (Ex. House, Vacation, Retirement)   _____

2. **When do I need the money?**

Within 1 Yr	_____
2 - 5 years	_____
5 - 10 years	_____
10 years or more	_____

3. **What am I Looking For?**
    - *Rank in order of priority 1, 2, o*

Safety	_____
Income	_____
Growth	_____

Step 2: What is My Risk Tolerance?

How comfortable am I with Volatility?

Check One:	
Not Very (Low Risk)	_____
Quite Comfortable (Medium)	_____
Very Comfortable (High)	_____

Step 3: What is my Asset Allocation?

Given my investment objective and risk tolerance, how much do I want to invest in:

Cash	_____ %
Bonds	_____ %
Stocks	_____ %
	100%

Step 4: How much money can I put towards this goal?

Total saved to date _____

Monthly contribution _____

Step 5: What is my plan of action for investing this money?

_____

_____

_____

WHICH INVESTMENTS ARE RIGHT FOR ME?

Step 1: What are my investment objectives?   Goal #3

    Ask yourself 3 Questions:
    1. **Why am I Saving?**
          (Ex. House, Vacation, Retirement)   _____

    2. **When do I need the money?**

Within 1 Yr	_____
2 - 5 years	_____
5 - 10 years	_____
10 years or more	_____

    3. **What am I Looking For?**
          - Rank in order of priority 1, 2, o

Safety	_____
Income	_____
Growth	_____

Step 2: What is My Risk Tolerance?
    How comfortable am I with Volatility?
          Check One:

Not Very (Low Risk)	_____
Quite Comfortable (Medium)	_____
Very Comfortable (High)	_____

Step 3: What is my Asset Allocation?
    Given my investment objective and risk tolerance, how much do I want to invest in:

Cash	_____	%
Bonds	_____	%
Stocks	_____	%
	100%	

Step 4: How much money can I put towards this goal?
          Total saved to date _____
          Monthly contribution _____

Step 5: What is my plan of action for investing this money?

_____
_____
_____

A Few Thoughts On Strategy

The basic information you have learned so far is the foundation upon which all investment strategies are built.

By learning the advantages and disadvantages of specific investment options, you gain insights as to why an advisor might advocate one over another for any one of your goals.

When you step back and look at your whole investment portfolio, there are a few over arching strategies that you want to see emerge.

Strategies You Can Use

Diversify. You may recall, diversification came up in the section on mutual funds. It is also a key strategy that should be applied to your whole portfolio, and isn't exclusive to mutual funds. The theory goes that if you have investments in multiple investment baskets, you won't go hungry if something radical happens to any one of your baskets. This reduces your overall investment risk.

Here are the four main ways that you can diversify:

Asset Classes If you allocated money into two or three asset classes in your plans, you have already diversified your portfolio. The advantage is that if there is a temporary dip in the value of your Stocks, your less volatile Cash or Bond investments can help cushion the blow. And if your safer investments are under performing, ideally your stocks will be showing positive returns.

Geographic Canada only represents 3% of the world's investment opportunities. You can benefit by spreading your investments across the US, Europe, Asia and Latin America.

Industry Different industries (Mining, Technology, Oil and Gas etc) yield different returns and some industries will peak while others tank. Choosing stocks, bonds or mutual funds in different industries is a good way to spread out the risk on higher risk investments.

Time Your GICs and Bonds can mature on different dates. For example, if you have $6,000 to invest, you may want to invest $2,000 in a 1 year GIC, $2,000 in a 3 year GIC and $2,000 in a 5 year GIC. If interest rates rise the next year, you'll have money available from the GIC that just matured to take advantage of the higher rate. And if interest rates drop when it comes time to reinvest, you will still have some money invested at the higher guaranteed rate. This is known in the investment world as *laddering*.

Invest regularly. The advantages of setting up a monthly investment contribution have been discussed before as well. But just to drive home the point, regular contributions do more than demonstrate your commitment to your goals. Investment theory says that if you buy investments consistently, in both good markets and bad markets, you spread out your risk and lower the average cost per investment. How? With any given amount of money, you can buy more when the market is low and less when the market is high. So all those shares you bought "low" more than make up for the few that you bought "high". This is known in the industry as *dollar cost averaging*.

Don't worry about timing the market. The amount of time you stay in the market has a much greater impact on your overall investment success than picking the exact right day to buy or sell. Your plans take your investment objectives and risk tolerance into consideration. There's no need to start speculating on timing, just get in there.

Re-invest your investment income If you can, any money you make in interest or dividends should be re-invested. That way the money you contribute and the income you make are both working for you. This is called the *power of compounding*. Many mutual funds will do this automatically.

Investment Tools You Can Use

Know when you will double your money If you want to know roughly how quickly your investments will help you achieve your investment goals, it is helpful to know when you could potentially double your money. To do this, use the *Rule of 72*.

Simply divide 72 by the expected rate of return.

If you expect to earn an average of 8%, divide 72 by 8.   72 / 8 = 9   So, 9 years to double.

If you expect to earn an average of 3%, divide 72 by 3.   72 / 3 = 24   So, 24 years to double.

When you look at the difference in how long it will take you to double your money, you can clearly see the potential advantage of investing in higher return asset classes. You can make more money faster!

Online Resources How to select your specific investment products is beyond the scope of this program but here are some online tools that will help you research your options. This kind of research is like window shopping; you don't have to spend a penny but you can dream about all the lovely options.

www.globeinvestor.com for researching Canadian and US stocks

www.globefund.com for researching Canadian mutual funds

www.morningstar.ca for researching Canadian mutual funds

your bank or investment company's web site will likely have investment calculators

Financial and Investment Education Money Coaches Canada offers a monthly financial education series, *Money Mondays,* held on the last Monday of the month. A wide variety of topics are covered to help you stay connected to your finances, to hear about major developments in the financial world and to learn more about investing and financial planning. Check out **moneymondays.ca** for more details.

Also check out **moneycoachescanada.ca** for newsletters, podcasts, tips, tools, resources and worksheets to help you continue to build your investment and financial knowledge and confidence.

Who To Trust With Your Investment Dollars

You now have enough basic knowledge to implement your own investment plan, but you don't have to. Approximately 90% of you will choose to work with an advisor of one kind or another.

When you decide to either work with someone, or to handle your own investing, make it a conscious and considered choice. Check yourself to make sure that you aren't abdicating or avoiding.

Some people avoid working with an advisor because they are afraid of picking the wrong person. Other people avoid investing altogether because they are afraid they will make the wrong decision. Stop avoiding - ask for advice or do some more research. Remember, you are here to take control.

The Do-It-Yourself Approach

Some people feel like they are the best captain of their ship and in this information age, you have unlimited access to information about specific funds, specific companies, market trends and more.

But do you have time? You might save yourself a few dollars in fees, and you might be more committed to your goals than anyone else on the planet, but if you are going to commit to managing your own investment portfolio, you have to make sure that you can make the time to really do it.

Are you really saving money? Yes you can avoid *some* fees, but you are adding a certain level of risk to the equation. Make sure you understand what fees even do-it-yourself investors have to pay and what service accompanies that fee.

Most banks and credit unions have *discount brokerage departments* that work well for do-it-yourself investors. You pay a smaller commission on buying and selling stocks and bonds than you would if you worked with a stock broker who provides advice and helps select investments for you. You can open an investment account and buy mutual funds, individual stocks, bonds or cash investments.

There are also web sites like **www.globeinvestor.com** that help you inventory and track your investments. These sites are free, and may give you more detailed information than your statement.

So, managing your own investments will take time and you are still going to pay some fees. When you look at that, you may decide that the added cost associated with an advisor is worth the money. Informed, trustworthy advice is worth a lot. And financial advisors really are a wealth of information.

Who Can Help You? How Can They Help? And How Do They Get Paid?

If you don't want to manage your own investments, there are a lot of different advisors to choose from. To pick the right advisor, you have to match your needs to the advisor's services, and make sure you will be able to work well together.
It used to be that choosing where to invest was simple. If you wanted a bank account or GIC you went

to a bank. If you wanted stocks and bonds, you went to a stock broker. Times have changed. We now have almost unlimited options, which is good, but it can take a bit of investigative work on your part. To start, be clear on *the amount you have to invest* and *your risk tolerance*. Go back to your Which Investments Are Right For Me worksheets. That information will help to narrow the field.

Your next step is to start asking friends and colleagues for referrals. But remember, they might have very different investment objectives, or they might require services that you do not. To be sure that you are getting a referral to the kind of advisor you want, it is important to understand what kind of advisors are out there, what they can do for you and how they get paid.

Bank Branches
Banks are a good place to start if you haven't invested before and have less than $50,000. (You also have the option of online banks.)

Banks now have licensed mutual fund representatives in their branches who can help you invest in mutual funds, GICs, Canada Savings Bonds, either within your RSP or outside your RSP. You can usually open a discount brokerage account through your local branch as well. Most branch staff are paid a salary and many of them are paid a bonus based on a variety of sales criteria.

Brokers or Investment Advisors
It used to be that most stock brokerage companies were owned privately. Now all the major banks have in-house brokerage operations and there are relatively few independent brokerage companies. Generally brokers, or investment advisors as they are more commonly called today, work with clients who have at least $50,000 - $100,000, and if they have been in the business for a while, this might be as high as $500,000 or more.

They research, advise and process investment trades on your behalf. Some investment advisors also provide financial planning services. You can buy virtually any investment or financial product through an investment advisor, including mutual funds, and they are compensated either by commission whenever they buy or sell investments for you, or if it is a fee-based account, the fee is a percentage of the investments they manage for you. Commissions depend on the price and quantity of the investments you are buying and selling, but it is typical to pay $200 or more per trade. Fees for "fee-based" accounts are generally between 1.5%-3% of the value of the investments that they hold on your behalf. For instance, if you have $150,000 invested with an investor advisor and their fee is 2%, you would pay $3,000 per year.

Financial Planners
A financial planner uses the financial planning process to help you manage all aspects of your personal finances more successfully. A Financial Planner will consider all of your financial needs including: budgeting and savings, debt management, tax planning, investments, insurance, retirement and estate planning. Many financial planners also provide investment management services and typically are paid commissions or a fee based on a percentage of assets if they manage your investments.

Fee-Only Planners and Money Coaches charge fees for their financial planning services and don't sell investment products. They may charge an hourly rate or a flat rate for a specific service. Because their income is not dependent on the amount you invest, or the type of investment you make, you can feel quite confident that they are giving you unbiased advice. Money Coaches Canada Coaches use this model.

Investment Counsellors or Private Investment Managers Investment counsellors, or private investment managers, deal with clients who have at least $500,000 and sometimes more. They offer highly specialized and personalized investment management services to their clients and they typically charge 1.0% - 1.5% of the value of the investments that they manage on your behalf.

It is important to keep in mind that there are also some advisors who work in very specialized fields. Some work in specialized areas of the market, such as mining stocks or ethical investments, some have minimum investment criteria for new clients, and others specialize in working with clients in particular industries. So when you ask a friend for a referral, also ask why they chose their advisor.

Fees to ask about

When you buy and sell mutual funds you may pay a sales charge, called a "load". Be sure to inquire about, and understand the implications of these sales charges before you invest.

Front-End Loads (FEL) These sales charges range between 0 - 5% of the amount of the initial investment. You pay this upfront commission when you purchase the funds and you may be able to negotiate the rate. The advantage of an FEL is that it is a fixed amount. You know how much money you have to invest, so you know the fee.

Back-End Loads (also called Deferred Sales Charges or DSC) You pay this fee when you sell your mutual fund. Back-end loads range from 1% to 8% of your investment and it may be based on the original purchase value of your investment, or the market value at the time of sale. This fee usually declines the longer you own the mutual fund, reaching zero after a period of years. Ask your advisor and read the prospectus for a schedule of charges as this will tell you how long you must hold the mutual fund before the back-end load reduces to zero.

No-Load Often banks and credit unions won't charge a fee if you invest in their own funds. You can also buy no-load mutual funds directly from the company that manages them. Companies like Phillips, Hager & North, Leith Wheeler, or Steadyhand offer no-load funds. But read the prospectus, sometimes no-load mutual funds have a minimum investment requirement.

Although not all mutual funds have a sales charge (e.g. no-load funds), all mutual funds charge a fee for ongoing management and administration of your investment.

Management Expense Ratio (MER): This is an annual fee charged by mutual fund companies to investors. It covers expenses such as investment management, marketing, accounting, administrative costs and fees to investment salespeople. MERs typically range from 0.05% (usually for lower risk investments such as money market funds) to more than 3% (usually for Canadian and international stock funds). You can find out about the MER in a fund's prospectus or by asking your advisor.

How to Interview a Potential Advisor

Finding an advisor who you trust, and who offers the services you need, can take some time and research. It's best to spend the time up front by interviewing 2 or 3 advisors. This is also a great opportunity to learn how advisors manage money, and to develop your confidence in the investing world.

Questions to Ask	**Answers to Listen For**
Can you describe the type of clients you serve?	Does the answer sound like you?
What are the costs of your service?	Understand the fees and commissions, if something is unclear, ask for clarification.
What products do you offer?	Are they the products you want to buy?
Do you have a minimum investment?	If so, do you have that much to invest?
What are your qualifications?	Listen for professional designations and amount of experience with clients like you.
How many times a year will we meet?	Once a year is usually ok for new investors.
How will I receive my statements?	You want to get regular statements so that you can monitor your accounts. And ask if they will help you interpret the statements.

You might also show them your investment worksheets and see what feedback they have for you. Bear in mind, advisors may have different strategies and they may have good reasons for suggesting alternatives. But listen to make sure that their strategy addresses your goals and that they can demonstrate the advantage of an alternate asset allocation.

You will likely learn a lot about the advisor from their responses. Be aware of how you are responding as well. The key to a good relationship is that you, the client, are comfortable.

It is a good idea to write down the information you get from the interview, make notes about their feedback, your response, and if you think you should take action on any items.

Do you work with an advisor currently? If so what kind? _____

How would you describe your level of comfort / satisfaction with your advisor?

_____

_____

Given your needs, what type of advisor would be best for you? _____

Remember, it's your hard-earned money that you are entrusting to your advisor. Make sure that you and your money are getting the respect you both deserve.

Review and Rebalance

Are your current investments going to adequately support
your goals and your new financial plan?   _____

Do you have the right overall asset allocation?   _____

Does it reflect your tolerance for risk?   _____

Do you have to make any changes?   _____

If so, take a moment to plan your next steps:

Do you need to ask people to refer an advisor? If so, who could you ask?

_____

Do you need to call your current advisor and set up a meeting to review your investments? If so, when?

_____

Are there investments or changes to your investments that you can make yourself? Which ones? How
will you make the changes? And when?

_____

_____

No matter what investments you choose, or who is managing your investments, you need to review your
portfolio at least once a year.

Change your investments when your life changes, not when the market does.

You may need to adjust your portfolio if you experience:

- a change in your life circumstances (e.g. get married, have kids, retire)

- a change in your goals

- a change in your risk tolerance

- a change in the time horizon for your goals

- aging. Younger people tend to hold more stocks or stock mutual funds, because they
  have time to ride out the dips. You may shift to a more cautious approach as you near
  retirement. After retirement, you will want to focus more on income investments because
  they will provide your monthly income.

You now have the basic framework to start investing with confidence. Be sure to take a life-long
approach to both investing, and learning about investing, but start today. Make a phone call or start
researching online. Go for it. Make your money work for you, and use it to live your best life.

Any other next steps for investing?

Investing is like fine dining.

Pairing is key. Red wine goes better with steak. White wine goes better with fish. Some investments are better with short term goals, and some are better with long term goals.

Taste is acquired. You are more likely to choose a wine that suits your palate if you know the characteristics of the different types of wine. Likewise, learning the advantages and disadvantages of different types of investments makes you better able to choose ones that suit your needs and your life.

Tastes change. You may enjoy French cuisine now, but as you age you might better appreciate the health benefits of Japanese cooking. Phases of life, and changes in priorities impact your investment choices. You'll make changes when you need to make them.

Bon Appetit. You don't have to be an expert to enjoy good wine, good food or good investments.

It's Tax Time

Understanding Income Tax

"Intaxication: Euphoria at getting a refund, which lasts until you realize it was your money to start with."

~Author unknown from a Washington Post word contest

This chapter is going to be short and sweet. It isn't a crash program in filing your tax return. The goal for this chapter is to get you thinking about how you are taxed on your income.

Once you understand that, you will be better able to talk to your financial advisor, or a tax specialist, to discuss specifically how you could factor taxation into your financial plan and reduce the amount of tax you pay each year.

Note: Taxes are different for everyone. In this chapter, you will learn basics that most people can apply, but you should always consult a tax specialist before making tax decisions.

Canadians are Progressive

In Canada, roughly the first $10,000 you earn is tax free. After that, it gets interesting. We have what is called a *progressive tax system*. Levels of income have been categorized into *income tax brackets* and higher income tax brackets are charged higher *tax rates*, or percentages of income due in tax.

The Federal and Provincial governments tax you separately but, unless you live in Quebec, you only file one form and pay one bill. The federal government applies its own tax rates to its income brackets. The provinces apply different rates to different brackets. To find out the tax rates for your province, visit the resource section of Money Coaches Canada's web site **www.moneycoachescanada.ca** or ask your tax specialist.

The key thing to remember about the progressive system, is that not all of your income is taxed at the same rate. To demonstrate this point, this example shows roughly how a woman earning $140,000 would be taxed in BC. You can use the same math, to see how you would be taxed at your level of income.

Asha is the Vice President of Sales at a resort company in Whistler, BC, making $140,000. She is taxed like this:

1st income bracket: $0 - $11,000
Thanks to basic personal and employment tax credits, Canadians pay no tax on the first $10,000 earned.

The first $11,000 she doesn't pay tax on

2nd income bracket: $11,001 - $44,000
Income in this bracket is taxed at 20%

The next $33,000 will be taxed at 20%

3rd income bracket: $44,001 - $88,000
Income in this bracket is taxed at 32%

The next $44,000 will be taxed at 32%

4th income bracket: $88,001 - $136,000
Income in this bracket is taxed at 41%

The next $48,000 will be taxed at 41%

Top income bracket: $136,001 and up
Income in this bracket is taxed at 44%

The final $4,000 will be taxed at 44%

$11,000	$33,000	$44,000	$48,000	$4,000	= $140,000 taxable income
x 0%	x 20%	x 32%	x 41%	x 44%	
$ 0	$ 6,600	$ 14,080	$ 19,680	$1,760	= $42,120 due in taxes

Asha is in the top income bracket, but the majority of her income is taxed at much less than the highest rate. Only the last $4,000 she earns will be taxed at 44%.

To find out what percentage of her income actually goes to taxes, divide the taxes due by the total taxable income.

$$\frac{\$42,120}{\$140,000} = 30\%$$

Therefore she takes home 70% of her income.

Note: Numbers have been approximated for illustrative purposes. CPP is not included in above calculations. See tax tables for accurate income brackets and tax rates.

Tax Talk

Total Income is all the money you earn including: salary, self employment revenue, bonuses and tips, investment income, and pension income. Asha's total income is $140,000.

Deductions in tax talk are expenses that the government allows you to subtract from your total income.

Taxable Income is your total income, minus tax deductions. This amount is used to determine which income tax bracket you are in.

Effective Tax Rate is the percentage of your total income that is actually taxed. Asha's effective tax rate is 30%.

Marginal Tax Rate is the tax rate charged on the last dollar you earn. Asha's marginal tax rate is 44%.

Pull out your most recent tax return or notice of assessment, what was your taxable income? (see line 260) $ _____

By dividing the amount you paid in tax by your total taxable income, what was your effective tax rate? $ _____

Using the tax tables on Money Coaches Canada's web site, what was your marginal tax rate?   _____ %

Why is it important to know your marginal tax rate?

1) You will know what rate of tax you will have to pay on any additional income you earn.

2) You will know how much tax you will save on anything you are able to deduct against your income.

Tax Planning

Plan to pay your taxes. If your taxes are not deducted from your pay cheque, and you have to pay a tax bill each year, don't let yourself be surprised by the amount. Once you know your marginal and effective tax rates, you can plan to save a sufficient amount of your income so that you aren't scrambling at tax time. Set up a savings account for your taxes and automatically transfer a percentage of your income each month.

Plan to pay LESS taxes. By knowing how your income is taxed, you can make decisions that enable you to retain more of your income.

Not All Income is Taxed Equally

Your pay cheque (or in the case of self-employed sole proprietors, your net business revenue) After the basic personal exemption, which is roughly the first $11,000 you earn, 100% of your income is taxable income and it is taxed according to the progressive tax rate system.

Your registered investment earnings (RSPs and pensions) are not taxed until you remove money from the registered investment.

Your non-registered investment earnings:

Interest on non-registered investments is fully taxable at your marginal tax rate.

So, if you earn 3% in interest on a $10,000 GIC, you will have earned $300. If your marginal tax rate is 30%, $90 of your earnings will go to tax and you only get to keep $210.

Dividend income from non-registered investments in Canadian companies qualifies for the dividend tax credit. As an incentive for Canadians to invest in Canadian companies, these earnings are given preferential tax treatment.

Capital Gains on non-registered investments Only 50% of your *realized* capital gains are taxed at your marginal tax rate. Some investments, such as stocks, bonds and certain types of mutual funds could *realize* capital gains in the year you sell. If your stock value goes up, but you don't sell, the gain is not *realized,* and therefore not taxed.

So, if you bought a stock for $1,000 and it grew to be worth $1,400 on the day you sell it, you would realize a gain of $400. But since only 50% of that is taxed, you only have to add $200 to your taxable income. If your marginal rate is 30%, you would only pay $60 in tax and you would get to keep $340.

Tax-Free Savings Accounts (TFSA) The federal government recently introduced a new incentive for Canadians to save and invest. When you save or invest money in a TFSA, the income accumulated will not be taxed. To give you a better understanding of this new kind of account, we have compiled a list of common questions about the Tax-Free Savings Account.

When was the TFSA introduced? Tax-Free Savings Accounts were introduced in 2009.

Who can contribute to a TFSA? Any Canadian over the age of 18 who files a tax return will be eligible to contribute to a TFSA.

Where can I set up a TFSA? Banks, credit unions and financial institutions offer TFSAs.

What types of investments can I hold in my TFSA? You can hold any type of RSP eligible investment including publicly traded stocks, bonds, mutual funds and cash deposits.

How much can I contribute to a TFSA? From 2009 to 2012, your annual contribution limit was $5,000 per year. The annual contribution limit is indexed to inflation in $500 increments. As of 2013, the contribution limit was increased to $5,500. Any unused contributions will add to your next year's contribution room. For example, if you have never contributed to a TFSA, then you will have $31,000 of available room in 2014.

Are contributions to a TFSA tax deductible? Unlike with RSPs, contributions are not tax-deductible.

Who keeps track of my contribution room? The Canada Revenue Agency (CRA) will track your TFSA room just as they do your RSP contribution room. Inquire by registering for "My Account" at **www.cra.gc.ca/myaccount** or by calling the CRA.

What are the Advantages of a TFSA?

- Investment income (such as interest, dividends and capital gains) earned in your TFSA will not be taxed. Your savings and investments grow tax-free.

- Withdrawals from a TFSA do not affect government benefits that are income tested such as Old Age Security (OAS), Guaranteed Income Supplements (GIS) or GST credits.

- You can withdraw money from your account at any time.

What should I use a TFSA for? A TFSA can provide additional savings for retirement and can also be used for shorter term goals such as saving for a trip, wedding or to buy a home.

Is it better to contribute to my RSP or to a TFSA? This is a tough question, as everybody's situation is different. Here are a few general guidelines that might help you decide. You should consider contributing to a TFSA if:

- you have already maximized your RSP contributions or have an employer pension plan that will meet your retirement needs

- you are in a low income year for tax purposes ($40,000 or lower)

- you want to save for something other than retirement, such as an emergency fund, house down payment, wedding or a new car

- you expect you will be in a very low income tax bracket at retirement (withdrawing from your TSFA account will not affect government benefits that are income tested)

- if you expect to be in a high tax bracket at retirement withdrawing from your TFSA for a large one-time purchase such as a new car or big trip will be more tax efficient than withdrawing from your RSP.

When can I withdraw funds from my TFSA? You can withdraw funds from your TFSA at any time and you will not pay tax on the income or withdrawal amount. In addition, the amount withdrawn from your account will be added to your contribution room for the coming year. This means you can reinvest the money that you withdraw at a later date.

Invest and Withdraw with your Taxes in Mind

Imagine the year is 2016. By now, Don and Sue have built up:

$40,000 in their TFSA accounts and $40,000 in RSPs

After several years of smart saving and investing, Don and Sue have managed to minimize the taxes they've paid annually, while building up a significant nest egg.

Now, they need $25,000 to pay for a new roof and minor renovations on their home.

They have a choice to make. They could withdraw money from their TSFA accounts or their RSPs.

If they use their RSP savings, they would have to withdraw over $35,000* to cover the $25,000 renovation costs and pay the taxes due on the RSP withdrawal (approximately $10,000). Also, their RSP contribution room would be lost.

By withdrawing the money from their TFSAs instead of their RSPs, Don and Susan save over $10,000 in taxes and they are free to re-contribute the $25,000 to their TFSA accounts at any point in the future. When they do, they can enjoy tax-free growth all over again. That's a smart choice.

* based on a calculation using a 30% marginal tax rate

You would be wise to consider the tax implications of your investment plans. If you have money in non-registered investments, it is important to note that safer investments tend to be taxed more heavily.

Go back and review your investment plans. How will those investment earnings be taxed?

You may be inspired to adjust the asset allocation of your portfolio if you can see a tax advantage to including some of the higher risk investments and some registered investments. But before you make any changes, remember that investment decisions should be based on your goals, your time frame and your risk tolerance.

Taxation is unlikely to effect your goals or your time frame. Does knowing how your investments will be taxed impact your risk tolerance? If so, go ahead and make adjustments, but if not, don't. Tax advantages can change with the government, investment decisions should only change with your life.

How to Minimize Your Tax Bill

Everyone's tax situation is unique, but here are three basic strategies to save on your tax bill:

Defer You can delay paying tax on money you earn today by investing in RSPs. The money you invest won't be taxed until you withdraw it. At retirement, your total income may be lower than it is today, and when you withdraw the money from the RSP it could be taxed at a lower rate than if you were to be taxed on it today.

The other benefit of deferring is that you can use the money that you would have paid in tax to purchase more investments or pay down debt. Deferring lets you use your money as long as you can.

Deduct Deductions help you effectively reduce your taxable income and potentially lower your marginal tax rate so you pay less tax. For example, the amount you contribute to RSPs can be deducted (subtracted) from your total taxable income, and so can eligible child care costs. If you are self-employed, your business expenses may also be deductions.

Tax credits don't reduce your taxable income, or your marginal tax rate, but they do reduce the amount of tax you have to pay. There are credits available for charitable donations, transit passes, medical expenses, tuition and even employment.

To make sure you are taking advantage of all the tax credits and deductions you are eligible for, check the Canada Revenue Agency web site. **www.cra-arc.gc.ca/**

Divide You can split your income with other family members in lower tax brackets. In retirement, there are advantages to pension splitting between spouses. You can also maximize your tax savings by claiming all of your medical expenses or charitable donations on one return. And if you are investing *outside of RSPs*, consider having the lower income earner purchase the investments, and have the higher income earner pay the bills. This way the lower income earner is taxed on the income from the investments at his/her lower rate.

For self-employed people, if you hire your spouse, or other family member, their salary can be deducted from your total taxable income, potentially lowering your marginal tax rate. Provided they are in a lower income bracket, their income will be taxed at a lower rate. The result is that more of the money you earn stays in the family.

Common Questions

Taxes are tough; there is no way around that. But you can use the information you just learned to save yourself money, have productive conversations with your tax and investment advisors, or at the very least, plan ahead for tax time. The examples on the next two pages run through answers to some frequently asked questions to further illustrate some of the key points.

If you have specific questions that you want to ask your advisor, make a note of them here:

_____

_____

Should I bother trying to earn extra money if I'm just going to pay more tax?

Jess works for a high tech firm as a programmer. A friend offered her a small side contract to build a web site. The contract will pay her $5,000 but Jess isn't sure if it is worth it, because she thinks she'll have to pay too much tax.

By knowing her marginal tax rate, Jess can figure out approximately how much income tax will be due on this additional income.

Current Taxable Income	$60,000
Additional Side Contract	+ $5,000
Total Taxable Income	$65,000

The marginal tax rate for this income level is 32% (approximated).

To calculate the additional tax due, multiply the additional income by the marginal tax rate:

$5,000 x 32% = $1,600 due

As a result of taking the contract, she will owe an additional $1,600 in taxes in April.

That leaves Jess with $3,400 from the contract, which is enough to fund her dream trip to Thailand! All of a sudden, taking the contract looks like a great idea!

I know that I should contribute to my RSPs for my retirement, but does it really save me money now?

Tony is a customer service rep earning $33,000 per year. He would like to make an RSP contribution of $3,000, but wonders how that decision will benefit him now.

Here's how it works:

Taxable Income Before Deductions	$33,000
The RSP is his only deduction	- $ 3,000
Total Taxable Income	$30,000

The marginal tax rate for his income level is 20% (approximated).

To calculate the tax savings, multiply the deduction amount by your marginal tax rate:

$3,000 x 20% = $600 saved

Because this deduction is the result of having bought RSPs, Tony will have to pay tax on the $3,000 when he removes it from the RSP, but until then, the $600 is his to do with as he sees fit. Maybe he'll buy more RSPs or use it to pay down his debt!

I'm self-employed, but is it really worth my time to save every receipt for deductions?

Jen is a self-employed life coach. She deducts her travel expenses, professional association fees, and a number of other business expenses, as well as her RSP contributions.

Taxable Income Before Deductions	$65,000
Total Deductions	- $15,000
Total Taxable Income	$50,000

Without the deductions she would have to pay roughly:

$11,000	$33,000	$21,000	=	$65,000 income
x 0%	x 20%	x 32%	=	32% marginal tax rate
$0	$ 6,600	$ 6,720	=	$13,320 due in taxes (approximate)

The business deductions will save Jen approximately:

$$\$15,000 \times 32\% = \$4,800$$

By using her deductions to reduce her taxable income, Jen will pay only $8,520 in taxes, saving her $4,800 on the $15,000 of deductions she claimed.

$4,800 would be almost a month's earnings - saving the receipts is worth a month of her time!

I have a regular job, is it still worth my time to look for deductions?

Gopal is an architect and a single dad. He deducts his childcare and his RSP contributions.

Taxable Income Before Deductions	$90,000
Total Deductions	- $20,000
Total Taxable Income	$70,000

Without deductions he would have to pay roughly:

$11,000	$33,000	$44,000	$2,000	=	$90,000 income
x 0%	x 20%	x 32%	x 41%	=	41% marginal tax rate
$0	$ 6,600	$ 14,080	$ 820	=	$21,500 due in taxes

Gopal's deductions drop him down from the 40% marginal tax bracket, to the 32% bracket:

$11,000	$33,000	$26,000	=	$70,000 income
x 0%	x 20%	x 32%	=	32% marginal tax rate
$0	$ 6,600	$ 8,320	=	$14,920 due in taxes (approximate)

Because his taxes are taken off of his pay cheque, at tax time he could receive $6,580 as a tax refund. And once you add in his tax credits for employment, and charitable donations, his refund could be even more. That certainly seems worth it!

Any other next steps for tax planning?

"Let our advance worrying become advance thinking and planning."

~Winston Churchill

"A good plan today is better than a perfect plan tomorrow."

~Proverb

"When planning for a year, plant corn. When planning for a decade, plant trees. When planning for life, train and educate people."

~Chinese Proverb

A Retirement Planning Primer

Your Future Depends on You

"The question isn't
at what age I want to retire,
it's at what income."

~ George Foreman

George brings up a key point about retirement. You can retire at any age, so long as you have the money to do it. Retirement planning factors in your age, your current lifestyle and expenses, your target retirement age, your goals for your retirement life, and your projected retirement income and expenses.

When you plan, you can change any one of the factors and see how it theoretically impacts the outcome. If you don't plan, you significantly increase the risk that come retirement, you won't like the practical outcome of the decisions (or lack thereof) you made along the way. You may think you are too young to be thinking about retirement, but it is never too soon to give yourself choices.

Retirement, or financial independence, ranks as one of people's top financial goals. But with so many immediate financial pressures, it is easy to resist or avoid thinking about the future. Remember, however difficult it is to do now, it will only get harder if you wait.

Retirement planning is a down payment on a tremendous gift - peace of mind.

The 3 Biggest Retirement Mistakes You Don't Want to Make

1. Avoiding the conversation

That conversation could be with yourself, it could be with a spouse, or it could be with an advisor. Having a conversation about retirement helps to bring some clarity to what your goals are.

2. Not having control over your expenses

It's not easy in light of all the competing demands for your money but learning to live within your means is critical for a comfortable retirement.

3. Carrying debt into retirement

It may not be avoidable, but carrying debt into retirement really limits your flexibility in the future. Aim to be debt-free before you retire.

A Framework for the Plan

Creating a retirement plan is a simple step by step process that will help you answer these questions:

- What does retirement mean to me and what are my retirement goals?

- How much money will I need in retirement?

- Where will my income come from?

- How much do I have to save now, to have enough in retirement?

This chapter will briefly address these questions, but it is a good idea to talk to your financial advisor about your retirement goals, your lifestyle, and the work you have been doing to plan for your retirement. Your advisor will then be able to address your unique needs.

What Does Retirement Mean to You?

Just as it was important to dream and set goals for your current life, it is important to do the same for your retirement so that you can build a financial plan accordingly.

Imagine what retirement will look like for you. It's different for everyone, so don't assume that you have to retire at 65 and take cruise ship holidays. Retirement might be the day you trade everything in to buy a pub and guest house in a quaint Irish village. Maybe you will transition from working to volunteering for a cause you have always wanted to support. Maybe you'll finally be able to go back to school!

Start with your dreams about retirement.

If money wasn't an issue, what would you aspire to do?   What future do you see?

Where would you live?   What would you be doing?   Who would you be doing it with?

Would you work?   How much would you work?   What is the source of your joy?

What contributions of money or time would you make ?   What legacy would you leave?

What
is your
vision of
retirement?

Will you
transition
slowly or
make a clean
break from
work?

Will you
stay in your
current home
or find a well-
maintained
condo?

Will you
travel?

Will your
family be
close by?

Will you work
part-time?

Will you
volunteer?

Will you ski or
golf more?

How prepared are you (emotionally, physically, financially) for retirement?

The next step is to set clear, attainable and true retirement goals, and then prioritize them. Again, you are going to write down the goal, the time frame for achieving the goal and an estimated cost. Don't worry about inflation, just write your estimations in today's dollars.

YOUR RETIREMENT GOALS

1. Retire in 10 years with an after tax income of $30,000 to cover your expenses

2. Pay off the mortgage within 10 years - $130,000

3. Start a home business within 5 years to bring in extra cash during retirement - start up costs $10,000

Your Retirement Goals	Cost / Value	Time Frame
1.		
2.		
3.		
4.		
5.		

Are these goals reflected on your goals worksheet? Should they be? Is your retirement a priority?

How much money will you need to live?

The next step is to figure out how much money you will need. There is no magic number. Just as visions are unique, the amount you need for retirement is unique.

Think about how much you will be spending monthly or annually when you reach retirement. The easiest way to estimate your retirement spending is to start with what you are spending right now and then think about what might change in retirement.

- Will you still have a mortgage or other debt?

- Will your children be grown and independent? Will you have to travel to see them?

- Do you or your spouse have health issues that could be a financial burden?

- Do you have travel plans, or dreams that you want to realize in retirement?

- Do you think you will want to stay in your house? Will you need to hire help?

Go back to your Cash Flow and your Spending and Savings Plan to see what you are spending today and then estimate what you think you will need in retirement.

Fill in the expenses of the Retirement Spending and Savings Plan on the next page, and don't worry about inflation. Just fill it in using today's dollars.

RETIREMENT LIFESTYLE EXPENSES

EXPENSES:

MAIN CHEQUING - Monthly Fixed Costs

	Monthly	Annual
Rent / Mortgage		
Condo/Strata Fees		
Property Insurance (if paid monthly)		
Property Taxes (if paid monthly)		
Gas or Oil (for heating)		
Hydro		
Phone		
Cable		
Internet		
Cell Phone(s)		
House Alarm		
Life Insurance Premiums		
Disability Insurance Premiums		
Health Premiums		
Vehicle Payments		
RSP		
RESPs		
Non-RSP Savings		
Bank Fees		
Vehicle Insurance (if paid monthly)		
Charitable Donation		
Clubs or Gym Membership (if paid monthly)		
Credit Card #1 Pymt		
Credit Card #2 Pymt		
Personal Loan / Student Loan Payment		
Line of Credit Payment		
Other		
Total Monthly Fixed Costs		

MONTHLY SPENDING - Chequing #2

	Monthly	Annual
Groceries & Cleaning Supplies		
Pet Food and Treats		
Pharmacy, Toiletries		
Gas for Vehicle		
Taxis / Bus/ Parking		
Snacks and Lunches at work		
Entertainment - Dining out, Movies, etc.		
Alcohol - (beer/wine) and/or Cigarettes		
Other		
Total Monthly Spending		

SAVINGS ACCOUNTS - Lump Sum and Annual Expenses

	Monthly	Annual
Fixed Annual & Lump Sum Expenses		
Property Taxes (if paid annually)		
Vehicle Insurance (if paid annually)		
Property Insurance (if paid annually)		
Clubs & Memberships (if paid annually)		
Magazine Subscriptions		
Costco Membership/Credit Card Annual Fees		
Professional / Accounting Fees		
Variable Annual & Lump Sum Expenses		
Home Repairs, Furniture and Household Items		
Vehicle Repairs and Maintenance		
Medical, Dental, Glasses, Contacts		
Personal Care (hair care, cosmetics, dry cleaning)		
Clothing, Shoes, Outerwear		
Gifts and Donations		
Vet Bills		
Travel, Vacations and Family Fun		
Self-Improvement & Hobbies		
Computer/Electronics		
Holiday Pay (if self-employed)		
Other		
Total Lump Sum and Annual Expenses		
TOTAL CASH NEEDS		

Remember to include the costs associated with your retirement lifestyle and costs associates with aging.

Where Will My Income Come From?

Now it's time to look at your potential sources of retirement income.

Employer Pensions: There are two kinds of employer pension plans.

Defined Benefit Plan

You and your employer contribute to a group pension that is professionally managed. In this way, the company takes responsibility for having enough money to pay employees a defined amount.

This provides you with a guaranteed monthly income at retirement, which is based on your employment income and years of service. This income is guaranteed for the rest of your life, and some or all of your benefit may be guaranteed for your spouse after your death.

Defined Contribution Plan

You and your employer make a specific contribution to your retirement plan each month or each year.

The accumulated savings is yours at retirement.

There are no guarantees on monthly payouts at retirement, or that the savings will last your lifetime.

The employee assumes the risk that the money is well invested.

The success of the plan depends on how much you and your employer contribute, how well the investments do and how carefully you draw down the funds at retirement.

Make sure you understand your pension plans, what your entitlements and options are in retirement, and how best to manage your plans today for maximum benefit.

Government Pensions Canadians may be eligible for the following pensions:

Canada Pension Plan (CPP)

The amount of your CPP benefit is based on a number of factors including the number of years you worked in Canada and the amount you contributed to the CPP over those years.

The maximum monthly pension benefit for 2014 is $1038/mo at age 65. That is over $12,400 per year.

You can apply to receive this benefit at 60 (the earliest you can), but your monthly benefit will be less than if you waited to start receiving it at 65. However, by starting it sooner, you might be able to leave your investments in the market for longer. If you apply to receive it at 70, your monthly benefit is higher than if you had started at 65. There is no financial benefit to delaying receiving your CPP past the age of 70.

Old Age Security (OAS)

The OAS is a monthly benefit available to most Canadians age 65 or older. Eligibility is based on your age and your years as a Canadian resident.

The maximum monthly benefit is currently $552 a month, or about $6,600 a year.

For more information visit **http://www.servicecanada.gc.ca/eng/isp/oas/oastoc.shtml**

Registered Savings If you don't have a pension, this may be your biggest source of income.

Registered Retirement Savings Plans (RSPs) are registered by the Canada
Revenue Agency and are designed to encourage Canadians to save for retirement. Contributions to an RSP are tax deductible at the time of investment. You defer paying tax on the money until you withdraw it from the RSP. RSPs can contain investments such as stocks, bonds, mutual funds, GICs, savings accounts.

You are allowed to contribute up to 18% of your previous year's earned income to your RSP. Any unused contribution room is carried forward indefinitely. Check your most recent notice of assessment from CRA to find out how much contribution room you have available.

Registered Retirement Income Funds (RIFs) When you decide to start drawing
a regular income from your registered savings, you are required to convert your RSPs into RIFs (or they must be converted by December 31st of the year you turn 71). Although the packaging for your investment changes, the RIF is the same money you accumulated in your RSP and possibly the money that was previously held in a Defined Contribution Pension, if you had one. Like an RSP, you can still invest in stocks, bonds, mutual funds, GICs, savings accounts, etc. Once you convert into an RIF, you must withdraw a minimum of 7 - 20% of the balance of the RIF each year. The minimum amount is based on your age at the time of withdrawal. Withdrawals are considered taxable income.

Spousal RSPs provide an opportunity to split future retirement income with your spouse.
The contributor takes advantage of the tax savings on the contribution, but the money is invested in the name of the contributor's spouse. Eventually when money is withdrawn from the RSP or RIF, the income will be taxed in the spouse's name, at their tax rate. This usually works well when the higher income earning spouse makes the contribution for a lower income spouse, thus maximizing the tax savings on the contribution and minimizing taxes payable when withdrawn later in retirement. It can also be used to even out expected retirement income between spouses to reduce the overall amount of taxes paid by a couple.

Note: The funds must be in a spousal RSP for a minimum of 3 years, otherwise monies withdrawn are taxed to the contributor. Recent government legislation allows for retired couples to split their pension income on their tax return, however, there are still some situations that make a spousal RSP an advantageous option. Talk to your tax or financial advisor.

Non-Registered Savings At retirement, you may have some investments outside of registered
accounts that provide you with an income.

Examples include: stocks, bonds, mutual funds, GICs, savings accounts, and tax-free savings accounts.

Other Income Use your creativity here. How else might you imagine earning income in retirement?

Examples include: Rental income, part-time employment, etc.

Estimating Your Income

Gather any pension statements that you have from the government relating to the Canada Pension Plan (CPP) and from your employer if you have a company defined benefit pension plan. These statements should give you an estimate of what you are entitled to at retirement. If you have been a resident of Canada for more than 10 years (after the age of 18), you will also be entitled to some if not the full Old Age Security (OAS) pension.

To find out how much you can expect to receive from CPP you can request what is called a CPP Statement of Contributions by calling 1-877-454-4051. There is also a link to order your statement online on the "Resources" page of the Money Coaches Canada web site.

How much income do you estimate you will receive annually from these sources?

Defined Benefit Pension Plan $ _____

Canadian Pension Plan $ _____

Old Age Security Pension $ _____

Other Income (rental, part time employment etc) $ _____

You will also receive income from your investments. This could include a defined contribution plan. It is much more complicated to calculate future income from investments. You will need to ask your financial advisor, or use retirement calculators (available on most banking web sites) to do an estimate. You will do an assignment using a retirement calculator. For now, write down what you do know.

How much do you currently have in:

Defined Contribution Pension $ _____

Registered Savings Plans $ _____

Non-Registered Investments $ _____

How much is currently being contributed annually to these sources:

Defined Contribution Pension $ _____

Registered Savings Plans $ _____

Non Registered Investments $ _____

How Much More Do I Have To Save? (Otherwise known as Gap Management.)

To find out how much you need to save for retirement, use the Financial Freedom calculator on our web site **www.moneycoachescanada.ca** in the "Resources" - UNSTUCK section.

You will need the estimated annual expenses figure from your Retirement Lifestyle Expenses worksheet and some of the income and investment information from the previous page to plug into the calculator.

The Financial Freedom calculator is required because your Retirement Lifestyle Expenses worksheet is in today's dollars and your income estimations will factor in: inflation, the estimated rate of return on your investments, when you expect to retire, and how long you expect your savings will have to last. (It is a good idea to run retirement numbers to age 95 to ensure that you don't outlive your money.)

Using the calculator you can see what happens to the numbers when you change one of the many factors (e.g. you can see the difference between how much you will need to save if you think your investments will average 4% growth or 6%, and that information might nudge you to look into different investments, or you can see how much savings you would need to retire at 55 instead of 65.)

It is possible that there will be a shortfall, or *gap* between how much money you estimate having in retirement (income) and how much money you think you will need to live the life you want (expenses). Don't be discouraged if there is a gap in your current plan. There usually is. The important thing is that now that you know about it, you need to plan for it and act on your plan.

5 Ways to Manage the Gap

1. Increase your savings for retirement. The best way to manage the gap is by saving more for your retirement. Take a good hard look at your current spending and earning patterns. Is there a way to earn more? Is there a way that you can trim back on certain expenses to free up a little more for retirement savings?

You've gone through this process before, so if you can't find any more money, promise yourself that if you get a raise or an unexpected windfall, that you will put some of the new money aside for retirement. And stick to your promise.

2. Improve your rate of return on your investments. If you are only investing in safer, lower interest bearing investments, there may be an opportunity to improve your rate of return with a different mix of investments. Talk to your financial planner or investment advisor about your portfolio or register for one of the Money Coaches Canada investing classes to get more detailed information about investing and retirement.

3. Revisit your retirement goals and time line. You may find that by working a little longer, or reducing your spending slightly in retirement, you can close the gap quite comfortably. Small changes like working 1-2 more years before retiring can make a significant difference to the success of your retirement.

4. Consider working part-time in retirement. A part-time job or home business will not only bring in added income, it will make your savings last longer and allow you to leave your money invested for longer.

5. Use the equity in your home. It is becoming more popular for seniors to stay in their home and use a loan on their equity for income. The benefit is that people can afford to stay in the family home for longer, the downside is that when it comes time to sell the home, you have to repay the loan, and there could be little equity left to move forward.

The old fashioned way to use the equity in your home is to sell your home. The equity you have built might be enough to bolster your savings *and* buy a less expensive property. Or you could opt to invest the entire amount, and use some of the investment income to pay rent.

If you plan to use the equity in your home at retirement, don't forget to factor in the loan payment and rent expenses into your Retirement Lifestyle Expenses worksheet.

Review, Revise and Take Action

What are you going to do to manage the gap?

_____

_____

_____

_____

_____

The work you have done in this chapter provides you with the foundation for your retirement plan.

Share this information with your financial advisor and make sure that your investments are supporting your retirement goals. If there are changes you can make now, make them. As soon as you do, you will be well on your way to enjoying a stress-free retirement!

Remember to review your retirement plans annually to ensure you are on track and make sure to update your plan with any significant changes in your goals or in your life.

Any other next steps for retirement planning?

Insurance Basics

What you might need & Why you might need it

Spend 1% of your life making sure you have a solid Plan B and 99% focused on living Plan A to the fullest!

So far, your plan has centered around your goals, essentially that's your Plan A.

But what if something should happen to you or your loved ones? It's time to spend a little bit of time on Plan B.

No one likes thinking about the potential for illness, injury, unemployment, or death but a good financial plan factors in your insurance needs. Neither planning nor insurance will prevent potentially difficult times. Being prepared can lessen the financial and emotional impact for you and for your family.

People have a lot of preconceived notions about insurance, and unfortunately about insurance sales people. Before you go any further, you will want to check your assumptions at the door. Use this chapter to fill in your knowledge gaps and take a positive approach to this aspect of your financial plan.

When you are familiar with your options, and confident that you can ask for what you want, call an insurance provider to help you assess your needs and help you select specific insurance products.

You Can Be Self-Insured

Before reviewing the types of insurance that you can buy, consider for a moment the possibility that you could be self-insured.

Being *self-insured* means that you have sufficient personal means to support yourself, and your loved ones. Full stop.

It means that if you, or your spouse, were unable to earn an income as a result of death, illness or injury, that your lifestyle, and the lifestyle of your dependents, would not be financially hampered.

In the event of a death, illness or injury, would you have sufficient means to:

pay off debt, so that your spouse or loved ones aren't left burdened with debt

provide income, so that you, or your dependents, can maintain the life you built and continue to save for the future

pay added expenses, for medical expenses, funeral arrangements, legal or tax bills

In our culture, many people live a little too close to the edge of their means. Based on your Spending and Savings Plan, you can figure out how close to the edge you are.

It is possible for people to build up sufficient savings, or to live a lifestyle that makes you independent of the need for insurance. But unless you, and your dependents, are in a position where there are "enough" personal financial means to cover your debts, lifestyle and additional expenses, you should consider purchasing appropriate insurance policies.

Get Your Money's Worth

Insurance premiums cost you money, so again, before you buy anything, you want to know how the purchase will be to your best advantage, and help you to live a life that is consistent with your values.

There are a lot of insurance products and policy options available to you. To make sure that you get the type of insurance, and the *amount* of insurance you require, think about the following questions as you review your insurance options and needs in case of illness, disability or death.

- How much money will you, or your dependents, need?

- What standard or quality of life do you want to support?

- What policies will give you the best coverage, for a price you can currently afford?

- Would you be better off with slightly less insurance and more savings, or the other way around?

The answers to these questions are different for everyone. Be sure to discuss them with a professional advisor who will take your whole financial plan into consideration.

Typical Times To Review Your Insurance Needs

You can buy insurance at any time of life, provided you have the financial means, and you meet the eligibility requirements. Listed below are times of life, when you would be especially wise to review your needs. (You may, or may not, need to make a change at any of these junctures, but thinking about your insurance, and other aspects of your financial plan at these key times is a good habit to get into.)

Buying a new home Often a couple buying a new house will consider buying life insurance policies. If either person in the couple were to die, or become unable to earn an income due to illness or injury, the other person could need financial assistance to make the mortgage payments and remain in the home.

Paying off your mortgage Once you are clear of major debts, and your shelter is secure, you may consider reducing your insurance coverage. Your living expenses are cut significantly when you stop having to make mortgage payments, so depending on the other circumstances in your life, you and your dependents, if any, may require less financial resources.

Making a life commitment If either you or your partner would be financially disadvantaged by the lack of the other's income, you might consider insurance at this time. However, if you both have a strong potential to earn, no dependants and no major debts to burden the other partner, you would need to weigh the cost of insurance against the benefits.

Getting divorced or losing a spouse You will need to adjust your policies if your spouse was the beneficiary. You may also want to look into forms of insurance that provide you with financial support if you become unable to take care of yourself or your dependents due to illness or injury. And if you received insurance coverage through your spouse's benefit plan, you will need to look at replacing that coverage.

Having children or other dependents Whatever the household situation, one parent, two parents or three, parents are wise to ensure that they have a financial back up plan to replace the contribution that they make to support their children, and other family members. Or, if you have an aging parent, sibling or someone who is financially dependent on you, you need to consider them when you review your insurance needs as well.

Having self-sufficient children or becoming dependent free When people no longer need you for their financial survival, your life expenses shift, so you might consider reducing your insurance. However as they age, some people look at life insurance as a way of securing a legacy, or even reducing the tax burden when their kids inherit their assets.

Starting or closing a business In either case, you will likely have specific insurance needs. And you may also require personal insurance to be eligible for certain financing.

Life Insurance

Just because everyone is going to die, doesn't mean everyone needs life insurance. That would be like arguing that everyone needs a burial plot - they don't. Some people make other arrangements.

Self-insurance is an example of an alternative arrangement to life insurance. Generally avoiding the issue is not an alternative arrangement, nor is it a good reason not to be insured.

The main reason that people buy life insurance is because their current income is supporting the lifestyle of people they care about; and without that income, those people would suffer financially.

You don't buy life insurance for yourself. You buy it for your beneficiary.

When the policy holder dies, the insurance company pays a lump sum to the beneficiary named in the policy. It is very important to keep this information up to date. If you have remarried, but your ex-partner is still named as your beneficiary, the insurance company has no choice but to pay your ex. If you name a child, and then have a second child, you may want to add both names to the policy. Or, if your beneficiary dies before you do, you will need to name someone else.

When choosing a beneficiary for your policy, try to imagine who will be financially responsible for your funeral arrangements, your debts, or your dependents.

In Canada, the money someone receives as a beneficiary of a life insurance policy is not taxable. So if you purchase a policy worth $500,000, your beneficiary should receive the full $500,000 when you die.

There are two basic forms of life insurance:

Term Insurance The sole purpose of buying term life insurance is to leave someone a guaranteed amount of money when you die. It is not a savings vehicle and it has no cashable value if it is canceled, or if it lapses.

> You purchase this form of life insurance in limited terms e.g. 5, 10 or 20 years.
>
> It is relatively inexpensive when you are young and healthy, but when you renew the policy, you are likely to pay an increased rate for each new term.
>
> Group insurance, provided as a benefit through your employer, is a type of term insurance that usually ends when you stop working for your employer. You may be able to convert your policy into private term insurance outside a group plan. Be sure to check rates and limits to new coverage.
>
> Mortgage insurance is also a form of term insurance. It is offered by most lending institutions and it pays the balance of your mortgage to the lending institution if a person listed on the mortgage dies. The premiums are set based on the amount of money you owe at the time of issuing the policy. But the value of your debt decreases over time. Therefore, the amount of insurance coverage that you are paying for decreases. However, your premium stays the same. It is often best to compare the cost of mortgage insurance to the cost of other life insurance options.

Whole Life / Universal Life Insurance

These policies have a life insurance component and an investment component. With each contribution, a portion pays for your insurance premium and the other portion is invested.

With a whole life policy, you pay level premiums for a specified number of years. In the early years of the policy, the chances that you will die are significantly lower. So, the premiums you pay exceed the actual cost of covering you. The insurance company invests these excess payments (on your behalf) to cover the increasing cost of insuring you as you get older.

With universal life, you choose the size of premiums and the payment period based on an assumed rate of return on the investments within the policy. Universal policies are said to have a *cash value*, because if you cancel the policy, any money that has accrued in your investments is yours to remove. (There may be a cancellation fee, or *redemption charge* added.)

These policies are often more expensive to start, but if you hold the policy long enough, you should reach a point where the policy has enough cash reserves to pay your future premiums.

This form of life insurance is often chosen by people who know they will need life insurance well into old age, for instance someone with a lifelong dependent. It may also be of interest to people who have maximized their RSP contributions because there can be tax benefits.

How do I buy Life Insurance?

Life insurance is available through insurance brokers or agents, banks and credit unions. You may also have, or be able to buy, life insurance through your company, alumni association or professional association.

How much does it cost?

Premiums for life insurance are dependent on your age, gender, health, smoking status, the term you choose and amount of coverage you want to purchase.

Currently, for a non-smoking, healthy 40 year old woman, premiums for a 10 year term policy of $500,000 would be in the range of $30-35 per month. For a non-smoking, healthy 40 year old male, premiums for the same type of policy would be in the $40-45 per month range. If all else is equal, life insurance premiums tend to be lower for women because we are expected to live longer, and the insurance company is more likely to keep its money for longer.

Who buys it?

Couples, parents, new home owners, and new business owners tend to buy life insurance, but it is important to remember that the amount they buy will likely change over the program of a lifetime. You may need more when you have a young family, no savings and/or a large debt. Typically, life insurance needs decline as you accumulate assets, and/or your dependents become independent.

If you are single, unless you have dependents, significant debts, or a burning desire to leave a financial legacy, you may not need life insurance. However, some singles do choose to secure life insurance coverage while they are young and healthy in anticipation of their future needs.

Disability Insurance

Most people hear a lot more about life insurance than disability insurance, but disability insurance is a very important type of insurance to consider.

The most valuable asset you have today is your *ability to earn income*. A disability could impede your ability to work, so the risk of illness and injury is a significant risk to your financial security.

Disability insurance can provide you with a monthly income if you cannot work.

So long as you are alive, you are going to need money, and if you aren't physically or mentally able to earn it, you need to know where it will come from. Personal savings is one option. Government assistance is minimal. Depending on family and loved ones might be an option. Disability insurance can pay as much as 85% of your current income, on a monthly basis.

But not all policies are equal so it is important to read the policy options carefully. Make sure you are clear on what constitutes a disability; how long you have to be disabled before the benefits begin; and how long the benefits will continue to be paid out.

Where do I get Disability Insurance?

Many employers provide some type of disability insurance, but don't assume it's included in your benefits package or that what is provided will be sufficient for your needs.

If you don't have sufficient coverage through your employer or if you are self employed, be sure to talk to a licensed insurance agent.

How much does it cost?

Disability insurance premiums are calculated based on a variety of considerations including: amount and term of coverage, age, gender, income, health, and occupation. Premiums can vary significantly from policy to policy.

To give you an idea, when Karin Mizgala was 41, she bought a disability policy worth $3,000/month (plus inflation) to age 65. She pays monthly premiums of $156. That may seem high, but if she was disabled at age 45, the policy would pay Karin $36,000 a year for 20 years, and cost the insurance company over a million dollars.

If you don't have a financial backup plan, you really need to consider the value of disability insurance.

Who buys it?

A lot of people buy it for a lot of different reasons. Single people buy it in the hopes of remaining self sufficient if they become disabled. Couples buy it so that neither person will have to bear the full financial responsibility for their household. Parents buy it to make sure they can continue to support their children and themselves. Self employed people buy it because they don't have company benefits such as sick leave and extended medical leave. Employed people buy it because their benefits may not include an extended sick leave, or their disability benefit might be limited.

> ### Did you know...
>
> Before the age of 65 there is significantly more risk of becoming disabled than dying.
>
> 3 out of 5 people will experience either a permanent or temporary disability before the age of 65.

The only people who are unlikely to consider disability insurance would be people who do not earn an income, or people who don't need to earn an income.

Tax considerations

The way your disability insurance premiums are paid determines how the government will tax you, should you ever be paid an income from the policy.

If you pay your own disability premiums, either directly to your insurer or your employer, any monthly benefits you receive will be tax-free.

If your employer pays your premiums, any monthly benefits you receive are considered taxable income, so if you have a policy that pays you $36,000 a year, you will have to pay taxes out of that income.

If you are self-employed, we recommend that you don't deduct your disability premiums as a business expense. If you do use the premiums as a deduction, you will have to pay tax on the monthly benefit if you ever need to make a claim.

Critical Illness Insurance

Critical illness insurance is still relatively new in Canada. It is designed to pay you a guaranteed amount of money if you become critically ill. Unlike disability insurance, your ability to earn an income is not an issue, your specific diagnosis is the issue.

What is a critical illness?

It is a good question. Oddly enough, different insurers, and different policies, may define critical illness differently, so review your options carefully. Generally speaking, a critical illness is a life threatening medical condition, such as life threatening forms of cancer, stroke or heart attack.

How does critical illness Insurance work?

Critical illness insurance pays out the full value of your policy in a lump sum 30 days after you are diagnosed, if you survive. This payment would not be taxable. You can use the money any way you choose. For example, you might choose to invest the lump sum and live off of the income, rest comfortably on a beach in Mexico, pay off debts, or pay for treatments or procedures that are not covered by your basic medical coverage.

Who buys it?

Critical illness coverage is becoming popular with single people because they are less likely to have someone in their life who could provide physical and financial support if they become critically ill.

Also, people who are ineligible for disability insurance, either because they are already disabled, or because they work in a high risk occupation, may still be eligible for critical illness insurance. Or anyone who foresees the need for cash, in the event of a critical illness.

You must be between the ages of 18 - 65 to qualify and you must have an acceptable medical history.

The more likely you are to experience a critical illness, the higher your premiums; and it is possible that you wouldn't be approved for coverage at all.

How much does it cost?

You can purchase any amount, from $25,000 - $2 million. Costs depend on your age, family history, smoking status, and medical history. The cost is also based on the number of critical illnesses you want covered.

Some policies give you the option to get your premiums back if you cancel the policy before using it. And some will pay out to your estate if you die before claiming. These options may have higher premiums.

Long Term Care Insurance

This is also relatively new in Canada. Long Term Care Insurance is designed to provide benefits to people who require private facility care, or home care, on a long term basis.

Currently, the average private, long term care facility costs approximately $100 a day, or $3,000 a month. That is significantly more than many people would otherwise budget for their shelter. Some home care is provided by the government, but many people who wish to remain in their home have to pay for additional care. The trend towards hiring professional caregivers means that people need to plan for significant health related expenses. Long term care insurance could be part of that plan.

How does Long Term Care Insurance work?

In order to claim on the policy, you have to be unable to perform two activities of daily living, such as: feeding, dressing, bathing, toileting, or cognitive activities. The benefit is expected to be tax free.

Who buys it?

People who do not qualify for critical illness or disability insurance might consider long term care insurance. People who have assets that are important to their family, like a family home, may be concerned about having to sell the asset should they need long term care. For those people, this insurance could provide assurance that they won't have to sell their assets. You must be over the age of 18 to purchase it.

How much does it cost?

Costs are based on the amount of monthly benefit you want, how long you want the benefit to last (term or lifetime), and whether or not you choose to have a monthly payment policy, or a reimbursement policy, meaning that you submit receipts for reimbursement. At this time, the insurance is so new, that companies are not guaranteeing premiums for more than five years.

What Are Your Basic Insurance Needs?

Everyone is different. These questions will help you start to consider your financial needs at death, or in the event of injury or illness. Refer back to your Spending and Savings Plan to see where specific costs might go up or down. In the event of a death, the rule of thumb for a couple or a parent with dependents, is that you will need 75% of the family's current income. In the event of illness or disability, your monthly expenses are most likely to go up.

How much income would you, or your family, need to replace?

If you die $ _____ per year   If you are disabled $ _____ per year

If your spouse dies $ _____ per year   If your spouse is disabled $ _____ per year

How much debt would you, or your family, need to pay off? $ _____

What additional expenses might you, or your family, need to pay?

If you or your spouse die: If you or your spouse are disabled:

e.g. funeral, child care, etc   e.g. medical assistance

_____   _____

_____   _____

Use the Insurance Inventory to compile information on the insurance you have.

You'll need to gather your policy documents, benefits booklets (and your spouse's) and possibly contact your insurance agent or the benefits manager at your work. List all the coverage you currently have.

Thinking about Life Insurance needs...

Ann is a stay at home mom with 2 infants. Her husband is the only income earner.

If he died, she would need:
$200,000 to pay off the mortgage
$40,000 annually for 10 years to cover her expenses, and save for her retirement and the kid's education.
$25,000 for the funeral, legal and other costs

Their insurance agent calculated that her husband would need a $577,400 term life insurance policy to cover her needs.

Thinking about Disability Insurance needs...

Joss and Sue both earn about $70,000. They have a son in school and a mortgage.

If either was disabled, they would still need to pay off the mortgage, pay for child care, cover their monthly expenses, save for the future, and pay additional health costs.

Both people have disability insurance for 60% of their current income. They are comfortable that that is enough to maintain a good quality of life.

YOUR INSURANCE INVENTORY

Life Insurance

Name of Person Insured You or Your Spouse	Annual Premium	Personal or Company Group Insurance	Type of Insurance Term, Universal, Whole Life	Amount of Insurance Coverage	Cash Value for Universal or Whole Life	Beneficiary Named	Insuring Company

Disability Insurance

Name of Person Insured You or Your Spouse	Annual Premium	Monthly Maximum Benefit	Taxable Yes/No	Benefit Period	Waiting Period or Elimination Period	Insuring Company

Critical Illness

Name of Person Insured You or Your Spouse	Annual Premium	Amount of Insurance Coverage	If the policy will payout to a beneficiary upon death: Beneficiary Name	Insuring Company

Long Term Care Insurance

Name of Person Insured You or Your Spouse	Annual Premium	Home or Facility Care	Benefit paid Monthly or by Reimbursement	Monthly / Maximum Benefit	Benefit Period	Insuring Company

Do you currently have any other forms of health related insurance? _____

Review, Revise and Take Action

The thing about insurance is that you *really never know* when you are going to need it. You don't want to be in a position where something has happened and you wish that you had gotten around to making a change or buying a policy, but you just kept putting it off.

Before you plan to buy coverage, review the coverage that you, and/or your spouse, already have:

Note any gaps in your coverage, or questions about your coverage. If you are part of a group plan at work, don't assume that it gives you all the coverage you require. Talk to the provider, or read your benefit booklet to make sure you understand your coverage and your benefits. If you or your spouse have personal insurance, ask yourself, and possibly your provider, if it is still the right policy for your current circumstances.

Review your named beneficiaries. Make sure all your policies have up to date beneficiaries named. If they need to be changed, mark that as an immediate "to-do" on your calendar.

If you decide that you need to buy insurance:

Find an agent you trust. Referrals are particularly important when it comes to buying insurance for a very simple reason. People dislike talking about death, illness and injury. That's not surprising. So look for an agent who puts you at ease. If you are comfortable with your agent, you will be that much more likely to call him or her when you need to adjust your policy.

Ask your financial advisor if s/he is licensed to sell you insurance. If so, it might be to your advantage to buy insurance from someone who knows your full financial story.

Ask how your insurance agent gets paid. Generally, you don't pay an agent, the insurance provider does. Some insurance agents receive a commission when they sell a product, and they may or may not receive a fee from the insurance provider after that. Be wary of an agent who regularly suggests new and better policies. If you have a policy that you know suits your needs, stick with it.

Manage your risks. This means making sure that you have plans (insurance or otherwise) to cover the greatest risks to you and to your family. Identify which types of insurance should be a top priority for you, and which you might add later. Keep in mind that your health could become an eligibility factor.

Update your Spending and Savings Plan. Insurance can be expensive, but it is often necessary to help you to live the life you want. So don't forget to factor it into your Spending and Saving Plan.

What changes will you make? What coverage do you think you need that you don't have currently?

Put Your Estate In Order

Estate Planning and Legal Issues

"And now, the end is near

and so I face the final curtain,

my friends, I'll say it clear,

I'll state my case of which I'm certain.

I've lived a life that's full,

I've travelled each and evr'y highway

and more, much more than this,

I did it my way."

~Paul Anka

Because you are building your own financial plan, you too will be able to say, you did it your way. Now it's time to face the final curtain, and tell people clearly what you want to happen when you die.

Too many people put this off. Why? You can't put off death. And you are way too far down the path to financial control to give up the ghost! Your job now is to plan and to protect those you love.

Okay, we have suggested you seek professional advice in other chapters, but we can't stress enough how important it is to get legal and financial help from estate planning professionals. We aren't lawyers, but as financial advisors, we have seen the family nightmares that can happen when estate planning is not properly considered. Save your family strife; plan and protect.

Note: There are unique tax considerations specific to estate planning. Talk to your investment and tax advisors to ensure that your plans factor in any taxes that might be passed on with your estate assets.

What is Estate Planning?

Estate planning may sound grand, but it just means that you have made plans for what you want to happen when you die, if you are incapacitated, or are near death. Essentially, it is a gift that you can prepare while you are alive, for the people or organizations that you leave behind.

Your *estate* is everything you own: personal effects, real estate, investments, insurance polices, intellectual property rights, licences and other business property, etc. Your estate also includes your debt.

It is critical that you make the necessary decisions and prepare the necessary documents now. If you don't, there may be no way for your wishes to be carried out. Worse yet, the legacy you leave could be a horrible financial and legal battle.

Key estate planning questions

- Who will be primarily responsible for carrying out your wishes upon death, or if you become unable to manage your affairs?

- Have you provided direction for your medical treatment, organ donation and funeral arrangements?

- Have you left enough money to cover your funeral expenses, or have you prepaid them?

- Does anyone know what type of burial and funeral arrangements you would like?

- Do you want to plan to die broke? Or do you want to plan to leave an income, or inheritance to loved ones?

- Do you have plans to cover any debts you might have?

- Who will inherit your estate? How will it be divided? Would you like to include a charity?

- Have you made special arrangements for any beneficiaries with special needs?

- Have you made special arrangements for children of a previous marriage?

- Do you need to make arrangements for someone to assume guardianship of your children?

- Do you have plans to transfer your business so that it survives after you die?

It might seem odd, but take a moment to journal what you would like to see happen when you die. Like everything else, you'll build your plan around your goals and visions for the future.

Start by writing about how you want to be remembered. Imagine how your financial decisions could contribute to that memory. You might want to answer some of the questions on the previous page, but this page is for you to *imagine your best exit.*

"Death,
the one
appointment
we all must
keep,

and for
which no
time is set."

Charlie
Chan

_____
_____
_____
_____
_____
_____
_____
_____
_____
_____
_____
_____
_____
_____
_____
_____
_____
_____
_____
_____

Make Your Wishes Clear

You need a will.

A will is a legal document that leaves instructions about what you want done with your estate.

It can save your family a tremendous amount of grief and headache. You may not think it could happen in your family, but the combination of intense emotion and money can turn even the most functional families into feuding, angry, monsters. The best way to minimize this risk is by being very clear and specific with your intentions upon death, and by having those wishes drafted into a legal will.

What happens if I die without a will?

If you die without a will, someone, usually a spouse or adult child, needs to file documents in the supreme court registry, asking the court to appoint him or her to settle your estate. If there is no one who can settle the estate, the public trustee takes responsibility and laws determine who will inherit. As a result, an estranged spouse, or a family member that you didn't know existed, could inherit everything.

The bottom line is, without a will you have no control over who gets what.

Where do I go to get a will?

A will can be drawn up by a lawyer, a notary public or you can do it yourself. However, we strongly encourage you to get a legal professional to assist you because it is imperative that a will is drafted, signed and initialed correctly; otherwise it could be considered invalid.

For most people, the cost of having a will drawn up is money well spent. But you can keep costs down by deciding the key points before seeing a legal professional.

Your will should clearly state: who will be the executor, who you will leave your money and possessions to, and if you have dependent children, who will be their guardian. Burial instructions can also be included.

Did you know...

Marriage nullifies a will, unless you specifically make it in contemplation of marriage. However, a divorce does not nullify a will.

A will is still valid even after divorce, unless you amend your will.

A new will automatically cancels any other will you had in the past.

An out-of-date will could cause as many problems for your family as not having had a will at all.

If you don't declare a legal guardian for your children, the court will choose one for you.

What assets are not included in my will?

Any asset that has a named beneficiary falls outside the jurisdiction of your will because you have already established who will inherit the asset.

RSPs, insurance policies, and pensions give you the option of naming a beneficiary. If a beneficiary is named, the asset is essentially spoken for.

If you have bank accounts, non-registered investments and real estate assets in joint names (with "right of survivorship"), at death, those assets should roll over to the other person named, so again, these assets don't need to be in your will.

And remember, it is up to you to keep the beneficiaries named on these assets up to date. If your will simply says that you want your son to inherit your estate, but your sister is still the named beneficiary on your RSP from the days before you had a child, you could accidentally give a large chunk of your assets to the wrong person.

Probate

Probate is the legal process that confirms the validity of a will. It takes time, and it costs money but in most cases it has to be done.

It is the responsibility of the executor to initiate the probate process. Though it can be done by the executor alone, it is a complicated process and is usually done through a lawyer.

Once a will has been through probate, financial institutions and the executor can begin the process of distributing the assets of the estate.

Unless the estate has minimal assets, it's not generally possible to avoid probating the will. While it may be desirable to avoid or minimize probate fees, it shouldn't be your only estate planning concern. However, people often plan to have some assets outside the will, such as life insurance policies, so they can go directly to the named beneficiary without delay.

Probate fees vary from province to province. Here's an example of how probate fees are calculated in Ontario:

Probate Fees in Ontario

Probate fees are calculated on the value of your estate, at date of death, in accordance with the following formula:

$5 for every $1,000 of the value of an estate up to $50,000

$15 for every $1,000 of the value of an estate over $50,000

So, probate fees on an estate of $350,000 would be $4,750. On an estate of $500,000 they would be $7,000.

Assets that have a designated beneficiary, (e.g. RSPs, pensions and life insurance policies) are not included in your estate for the purpose of calculating probate fees.

Who Will Speak For You When You Can No Longer Speak For Yourself?

The Executor

An *executor* is the person you appoint to carry out the instructions of your will. You could choose a family member, a trusted friend, a business partner, or a professional (e.g. your lawyer). You could also choose an institution, such as a trust company.

Ideally, you want to choose someone who is likely to outlive you, and who lives in your city or town, so that various administration duties don't require that person to make multiple or long journeys. Also, this is a diplomatic, and detail oriented job. Depending on your family dynamics, you may be able to count on a specific family member, or you may see advantages to asking someone outside the immediate family to take the role. An executor can be paid a fee, you can stipulate this specifically in your will, or the executor can claim up to 5% of the estate value with the permission of the beneficiaries.

The duties of the executor include:

- completing your funeral arrangements

- having the will probated and distributing assets to your beneficiaries

- paying your debts

- completing your income tax return and applying for the Canada Pension Plan death benefit

Financial Power of Attorney

A will only becomes valid upon death. But what happens if you are incapacitated and can't handle your financial affairs? Even if you are married, your spouse can't just step in unless your accounts or real estate are in joint names.

A Power of Attorney allows someone to make financial decisions for you, and sign financial documents on your behalf, if you are unable to do so due to accident, illness, or absence. Without a legal declaration, no one, not even your spouse or your parents, can sign for you.

What you need to know about a Power of Attorney to protect yourself:

- it can be limited to certain assets or to a specific period of time

- it does not cover personal care or medical decisions

- it takes effect immediately upon signing

- it ceases on death, or if it is revoked, or in the case of a "time limited" Power of Attorney, on a specified date.

A Power of Attorney is a powerful document that gives the person you appoint significant rights and responsibilities. Unless your attorney is your spouse, it's best to keep your Power of Attorney document with your lawyer, with instructions to release the document to your appointed attorney only if medical or other pre-stated conditions are met. You may want to appoint two people to act as 'co-attorneys' to avoid potential abuses, but make sure you pick two people who can work together.

Health Care Directive

Depending on where you live in Canada, your wishes for your medical care should you become too ill or incapacitated to make decisions for yourself can be outlined in a Living Will, Representation Agreement, Power of Attorney for Personal Care, Advance Health Care Directive or similar document. Without such advance planning and appropriate documentation, decisions concerning your body and life could be made by people who don't know, or don't respect, your wishes. If you're in a medical situation where you are considered by medical staff to be unable to make decisions about your care, by law, they have to ask your family for instruction.

If you have no family, decisions about your care will go before the Public Guardian and Trustee unless you have legally named a representative. Make sure you know the laws for your province and ensure that you have the legal documentation you need to ensure decisions about your health and personal care are made by the person you choose.

For example, if you want to ensure that no extraordinary measures are used to keep you alive (if in a coma or dying from a terminal illness), you need to make sure that the representative you name will have the legal authority to see your wishes are followed.

Being clear about your wishes, and who you trust to speak for you, can prevent serious family disputes over medical treatment decisions.

Talk While You Still Can

It may be difficult to talk to people about your plans, but it is much better for everyone if you do.

Ultimately, you want decisions about your assets, your medical treatments and potentially your death, to be your own. And it is important to recognize that it could be difficult for family members to fully appreciate your wishes if they are in crisis. So talking and writing a clear plan now gives you an opportunity to address their concerns and express your point of view.

Tell the appropriate people where your financial and legal documents are kept. Make sure they know who your lawyer and financial advisors are. If people don't know you have made plans, the plans won't do you much good, unless your lawyer just happens to attend your bed side.

If you are named in someone else's estate plan (your partner, children, or parents) make sure you understand your responsibilities and that you talk to them about their wishes, so you can respect them.

Further Research

If you want to do a bit more research on the legal and financial aspects of Estate Planning, including probate fees in your province, these web sites have a wealth of information:

www.legalline.ca

www.taxtips.ca/willsandestates/probatefees.htm

www.publiclegaled.bc.ca

www.nidus.ca

www.yourlegalrights.on.ca

www.justice.alberta.ca

CLARIFY AND COMMUNICATE YOUR WISHES

Do you presently have a will?   YES / NO

Where do you keep it, or plan to keep it?   _____

Who have you named as Executor?   _____

Who have you named as alternate Executor?   _____

Who would you like to name as the Executor?   _____

Who would you like to name as the alternate Executor?   _____

Have you talked to your Executor(s) about your wishes?   YES / NO

Who should your Executor call for help with your legal affairs?   _____

Does your executor know where to find your will,
and know the contact information for your lawyer?   YES / NO

Who should your Executor call for help with your financial affairs?
                                                                                       _____

Does your executor know where to find your financial records,
and know the contact information for your financial advisor?   YES / NO

If needed, who have you named to be Guardian of your children? _____

If needed, who have you named as the alternate Guardian?   _____

Who would you like to name as the Guardian of your children?   _____

If needed, who would you like to be an alternate Guardian?   _____

Have you talked to the potential guardian about this wish?   YES / NO

Financial Power of Attorney

Have you prepared documents to assign someone Power of Attorney?   YES / NO

Who have you named?   _____

Who would you like to name?   _____

Have you talked to the person about your wishes?   YES / NO

Where are the documents? Or where do you plan to keep them?   _____

Health Care Directives

Do you have a Representation Agreement or Power of Attorney for personal care?   YES / NO

Do you have a Living Will?   YES / NO

Where are the documents, or where do you plan to keep them?   _____

Are you an organ donor?   YES / NO

Does your family know about your plans?   YES / NO

Other information you should share with your estate planning advisor, and your representatives:

Were you married previously?   YES / NO

Do you have children from a previous marriage?   YES / NO

Are you presently named as executor, trustee, or guardian in any wills?   YES / NO

Are you guarantor or co-signer for any loans?   YES / NO

Are you presently involved in any legal suits?   YES / NO

Do you presently receive, administer, or contribute to any trust agreements?   YES / NO

Do you hold Power of Attorney on anyone's behalf?   YES / NO

Your Estate Planning Action Plan

List the actions you need to take to ensure your estate plans are complete and up to date.

_____

_____

_____

_____

_____

_____

_____

Take Action
It is Your Life, and Your Money

"Dreams pass into the reality of action.
From the action stems the dream again;
and this interdependence
produces the highest form of living."

~Anais Nin

Ready or not, you've reached the final chapter. How do you feel? Confident? Scared? Secure? Empowered? Confused? Elated? All of the above? That would be about right.

Now you don't have to feel like an expert, you aren't one. You don't even have to have everything under control yet. But as this program draws to a close, you need to promise yourself that you will keep working on your plan, you will keep asking questions, and most importantly, you will keep control of your money.

Each time you dream a new dream, or a new opportunity presents itself in your life, you can use what you have learned here to systematically ensure that your money will support you to live your best life.

As Anais Nin says, the cycle of turning dreams into action and action into new dreams is continuous. You made your plans and you can make new ones when the need presents itself. Likewise, it is up to you to take the appropriate, conscious action to make your dreams a reality.

Stand Firmly On Your Accomplishments To Reach Your Goals

To create the life you want, it is important to have goals and to look into the future to see yourself achieving those goals. But it is equally important to look back, and to take strength from how far you have come. If you only ever look towards what you want, you risk overlooking what you have.

Look what you've accomplished so far:

- you are clear about your **Dreams** and your **Goals**

- you know what you are willing (and not willing) to do to achieve them

- you have a better awareness of your **Relationship To Money**

- you know that your **Net Worth** statement is a snapshot of your finances at a given point in time

- you also know that your **Net Worth** is the result of your past financial choices, and that you have the tools, and the know-how, to make more empowered choices in the future

- you have a **Spending & Savings Plan** and the work you have done to date means you can be confident adjusting it when additional needs or wants come up

- you have started your **Investment Plan,** and you know what kinds of investments are right for your goals

- you are familiar with the various financial advisors who can help you get where you want to go, and you have your own plan

- you are ready to delegate and not abdicate responsibility

- you have started your **Retirement Plan**

- you have a better understanding of the **Canadian tax system**

- you are familiar with different types of **Insurance** and have reviewed your individual needs

- you know why you need an up-to-date will, power of attorney, and health care directive; and you have already started your **Estate Plan.**

How much money have you saved since starting this program? $_____

How much debt have you paid down since starting this program? $_____

That is a long list of accomplishments.

Use everything you have learned, all the decisions you have made, to build your financial confidence. And when you look forward to the goals you want to achieve, know that you have already done a tremendous amount of work. Use that energy to keep yourself on track and focused on your success.

Take Conscious Action Now

We have given you tips and tools to help you get organized and focused, but only you can take the *conscious action* required to live your best life.

You are taking conscious action when you:

- review your plan and act on your intentions

- ask questions and further your financial education

- check-in with yourself, and exercise your awareness

- spend and save your money with intention, education and awareness (every single day).

It's one thing to learn the basics of financial planning, but it's another thing to follow through and move your plans into action.

What final steps do you need to take to complete your financial plan? Review this learning guide one more time. Have you completed all the assignments? Do you have action items at the end of the chapters left to complete? Are there phone calls, or appointments, you need to make to follow through on your plans?

Once you have reviewed the work you've done so far, complete the Your Money Map Checklist on the next page so that you have a quick reference of what you have done, and what you have left to do.

And use the Action Plan page to consolidate your to-do lists. List anything you need to do to complete your plan, or to move your plan into action. The key to the Action Plan is to be specific and set deadlines for yourself. You may even want to put your Action Plan up on your fridge, or keep a copy of it in your day timer to remind you of your to-do's.

"A little knowledge that acts
is worth infinitely more than
much knowledge that is idle."
~Kahlil Gibran

YOUR MONEY MAP CHECKLIST

	Yes	No	Don't Know
1. Have you written down your Life and Financial Goals?	☐	☐	☐
2. Do you know what your Net Worth is?	☐	☐	☐
3. Have you prepared your Spending and Saving Plan?	☐	☐	☐
4. Are you regularly contributing savings towards your goals?	☐	☐	☐
5. Do you have an emergency fund or personal line of credit?	☐	☐	☐
6. Do you pay your credit cards in full every month?	☐	☐	☐
7. Do you have an investment strategy that is appropriate for your goals and your risk tolerance?	☐	☐	☐
8. Do you understand how to read your investment statements? (If not, now is the time to book an appointment with your advisor!)	☐	☐	☐
9. Are you saving for your retirement every year?	☐	☐	☐
10. Are you on track for your retirement goals?	☐	☐	☐
11. Are you confident that you are taking advantage of all the tax deductions that you are entitled to?	☐	☐	☐
12. Do you have adequate life insurance?	☐	☐	☐
13. Do you have adequate disability and/or critical illness insurance?	☐	☐	☐
14. Are your beneficiaries up to date on your RSPs, pensions and insurance policies?	☐	☐	☐
15. Do you have a good understanding of your pension and insurance programs with your employer?	☐	☐	☐
16. Do you have an up to date will, power of attorney and health care directive?	☐	☐	☐
17. Do you know what you need to do to achieve your financial goals?	☐	☐	☐

ACTION PLAN

If you answered No or Don't Know to any of the questions on the Your Money Map Checklist you will need an Action Plan to achieve your goals. Your Action Plan should be very specific with a time frame assigned to each item on your list.

Action Step   **Time Frame**

☐ _____   _____

☐ _____   _____

☐ _____   _____

☐ _____   _____

☐ _____   _____

☐ _____   _____

☐ _____   _____

☐ _____   _____

☐ _____   _____

For example:

√   Review my action steps in each section   Today

√   Schedule in my day timer an hour a month to work on finances   Today

√   Set up a savings account for my priority goals   Monday on my lunch break

√   Book an appointment with my investment advisor to   By Friday
    review investments and to increase my RSP contribution

    Update my will   By December 31

    Find a friend to keep me motivated,   Before New Year
    and on track with my finances

    Continue to learn about finances   Ongoing!

Review and Revise

You had an opportunity to review and revise at the end of many of the chapters. In most cases, there was a suggestion made as to how often you should review the work you did, and the plans you made.

As a general rule, just keep in mind that you need to review and revise your plans to address your changing needs, goals, and overall financial position. This is especially important if you have significant changes in your life, such as marriage, divorce, having children, or retirement.

At the end of this chapter is a quiz called My Annual Review Checklist. You can take it annually, either at the end of the year, at tax time, or whenever you do your goal setting for the year. Use it as a guide to make sure you are staying on track.

Keep Up the Good Work

Momentum is a great thing. Once you start to move, momentum helps to keep you moving in the right direction. Maintain the momentum you've built up with some of the following strategies:

Schedule an hour a month for your money. It really isn't very much time in the whole scheme of things, but it can be the difference between staying focused and using your money to achieve your goals, and falling back into familiar, but not-so-fabulous habits. Use the time to review what you have learned, review your goals, look up investing information, or to make sure you are sticking to your Spending and Savings Plan.

Find financial friends. Once you complete the program, you may find that you would like to talk to others about what you have learned. Sharing what you have learned helps you to continue to learn and keeps the information fresh in your mind. Consider mentoring other people to use their money to live their best life - what better gift? And when you start asking your friends about their financial know-how, you might be surprised at what valuable information they have to share with you.

Read a book. Here's a list of books that Sheila and Karin personally recommend:

UNSTUCK: How to Get Out of Your Money Rut and Start Living the Life You Want - Karin Mizgala and Sheila Walkington

Debt-Free Forever - Gail Vaz-Oxlade

The Empowered Investor: A Guide to Building Better Portfolios - Keith Matthews

Money, a Memoir: Women, Emotions and Cash - Liz Perle

Rob Carrick's Guide to What's Good, Bad and Downright Awful in Canadian Investments Today

The Financially Empowered Woman: Everything You Really Want to Know About Your Money - Tracy Theemes

Smart Women Finish Rich: 9 Steps to Creating a Rich Future - David Bach

Moolala: Why Smart People Do Dumb Things With Their Money (and What You Can Do About It) - Bruce Sellery

The Soul of Money: Transforming Your Relationship with Your Money and Life - Lynne Twist

The Wealthy Barber Returns - David Chilton

You Can't Take it With You: Common Sense Estate Planning for Canadians - Sandra Foster

Your Money or Your Life - Vicki Robin

Your Retirement Income Blueprint - Daryl Diamond

Do some online research.

Money Coaches Canada
www.moneycoachescanada.ca

Money Mondays
www.moneymondays.ca

Canada Customs & Revenue Agency (tax information)
www.cra-arc.gc.ca/

Financial Planning Standards Council (find certified financial planners)
www.fpsc.ca

Globe & Mail (articles on the markets, mutual funds, stock quotes, etc.)
www.globeinvestor.com

Investment Funds Institute (education)
www.ific.ca

Morningstar Canada (mutual fund rankings)
www.morningstar.ca

Responsible Investment Association (ethical investing)
www.socialinvestment.ca

Continue to learn. We know how challenging it can be to stay motivated and on track with your money, so we have created an opportunity to connect with your local Money Coach regularly. *Money Mondays* are held on the last Monday of the month and are a great way for you to stay connected to your finances, and to get to know what money coaching is all about. Check out **moneymondays.ca** for more details. Also be sure to visit **moneycoachescanada.ca** to take advantage of the programs, events and resources to continue to grow your financial wisdom and confidence.

Stay in touch. You may have completed Your Money Map, but you remain an important part of the Money Coaches Canada network. You are officially Alumni! Drop us a line to let us know how you are doing. Or stay connected to us and other alumni through our newsletters, special events and other workshops. When you need it, our Money Coaches are available for further one-on-one financial coaching, retirement planning or family financial coaching. Bottom line, we are here to continue to support you to stay on track with your plan.

Remember the Secret

At the very beginning of this program we told you the secret to your financial success. Do you remember what it is?

The real key to financial satisfaction is aligning the money you have (and will have) with your values, aspirations and goals.

You know what you want. You have a plan to get it. You know what obstacles you have faced in the past, and you know what obstacles other people face. And you know that people take control of their finances everyday.

Use that knowledge to keep yourself on track.

Believe it or not, following your plan is the easy part, provided you don't start telling yourself stories like, "it isn't really that important to me", or "I'll save next month", or "I'm not getting anywhere".

You know so much more today than you did at the start, you have already gained so much, and come so far. Sometimes your money just needs a chance to catch up to you. And it will.

Starting now, you:

- use your money to achieve your goals and

- use your goals to motivate you to keep control of your money.

And so it goes. You can definitely do this. You've already begun!

"My will shall shape the future.
Whether I fail or succeed shall be no man's doing but my own.
I am the force; I can clear any obstacle before me or I can be lost in the maze.
My choice; my responsibility; win or lose, only I hold the key to my destiny."
~Elaine Maxwell

MY ANNUAL REVIEW CHECKLIST

(To be completed a year after completing the program, and annually after that.)

☐ **Review and revise your life & financial goals**
Have major life events changed your goals?
How far have you come?

_____

_____

☐ **Update your Net Worth Statement**
Has your Net Worth improved since last year?
Why or why not?

_____

_____

☐ **Update your Spending and Savings Plan**
Are you following your Spending & Savings Plan?
What have been the challenges? Successes?

_____

_____

☐ **Review your savings for your priority goals**
Are you regularly contributing to your savings as planned?
Are you satisfied with how much you have saved for your goals?
Could you contribute more now?
Do you have an emergency fund?

_____

_____

☐ **Review your debt**
Are you debt-free?
Do you have a date that you want to be debt-free?
Are you paying your credit cards in full every month?
Are you paying down your debt as you had planned?

_____

_____

☐ **Update your investment inventory and review your asset allocation**
Are you investing as planned?
Is your asset mix still appropriate for your goals?

_____

_____

☐ **Review your Retirement Plan**
Are you clear about what you need to save for retirement?
Are you saving enough to meet your retirement goals?
How much do you have in your Pension or RSP now?
Are your named beneficiaries up to date on your Pension and RSP?

_____

_____

☐ **Meet your financial advisor to review your investments**
Have your found an advisor you like working with?
Are you on track with your investment goals?
Are you on track with your retirement goals?
Do you need to rebalance or adjust your asset allocation?

_____

_____

☐ **Review your insurance policies**
Do you have adequate life insurance?
Are your beneficiaries up to date on your life insurance?
Do you have adequate disability insurance to cover your lifestyle and savings needs should you
become disabled or unable to work due to illness?

_____

_____

☐ **Review your Estate Plan**
Do you have an up to date will, power of attorney, health care directive?

_____

_____

Thank you!

Our Best Wishes

for Your Personal and

Financial Growth.

The Money Coaches Canada Team

CPSIA information can be obtained at www.ICGtesting.com
Printed in the USA
LVOW02s2249050614

388809LV00001B/1/P

9 780991 705412